Tales from a Hostel at the Edge of the World

jbecan@hotmail.com

Tales from a Hostel at the Edge of the World

To Corinne and Sabrina,
my Favorite Ghostesses!
I love you guys and I love your podcast. I have a few good stories of my own and I feel that sending you these books is the best way to share them.

Jeff Becan

See you on chapter 20!

- Jeff

© 2021

ISBN: 979-8-74469-267-4

Dedicated to the best damn hostel in the universe and to all of those who graced it

with your presence. Thank you.

With honor and respect.

Contents

Prologue: The Idea   i

1. A Cold Windy Island   1
2. Opening Day   5
3. A Dark and Stormy Night   9
4. Good Times Ahead   13
5. Born Again Christians   19
6. The Mystifying Oracle   25
7. Bad Eggs   31
8. A Day in the Life   41
9. Strange Birds   49
10. Bending the Rules   59
11. Season's End   67
12. The Fall and the Rise   71
13. Turbulence   77
14. Something About Mary   81
15. The Best of Times   85
16. Return of the Plumber   91
17. Cimex lectularius   97
18. The Story So Far   103
19. Halcyon Days   111
20. The Other Side   117
21. Starry Nights   125
22. August   129
23. Thanksgiving   135

Afterword   139

Prologue: The Idea

In which our narrative begins with an homage to the world of travel by hostels and why I wanted to run one.

If we define a hostel as a simple, inexpensive lodging place for travelers, then my best guess is that the very first hostels were probably found in caves. Traversing the wilds in search of big game, early humans in new territories would certainly have had need of temporary shelter, and I can easily envision routes of cave-hostels catering to this demographic. For the mere price of a shank of sabretooth tiger, your average nomad could probably throw his or her pelts down on the floor and rest assured that the hosts would likely allow them to wake up alive in the morning. In order to be competitive, some of these hostels may have even advertised brand new cave paintings and state of the art communal fires. Continental breakfasts were probably not included.

But this is just idle speculation. What we do know is that the word 'hostel', which can be roughly translated as 'house of lodging', can be traced back to Middle English, which can be traced back to Early French, which can be traced back to Medieval Latin. This makes sense because Medieval Europe in the eleventh and twelfth centuries had been the old stomping grounds of the 'wandering scholars', vagabond students who traveled from university to university, finding temporary lodging in monastery dormitories along the way.

I think that we can safely go back even further than that, however, if we take as evidence the ancient Irish epic known as *The Destruction of Da Derga's Hostel*. This gripping tale of kingly leadership, feuds, curses and battles (which, spoiler alert, culminates in its title), was transcribed by Irish monks as early as 1100 AD, and had certainly been passed down orally for many generations before that.

According to most accounts, however, the modern 'youth hostel movement' began in Germany on the cusp of the nineteenth and twentieth centuries. Pioneered by a schoolteacher named Richard Schirrmann, it was originally intended as a scouting organization of sorts, a means by which young boys and girls could escape the stifling environments of their industrialized cities, escape to the great outdoors, breathe free, and trek from hostel to hostel for days on end.

At that time and place, groups of children hiking through the countryside wearing rucksacks on their backs and sporting comfortable clothing was a radical concept, but the idea was to spread like crazy. The first hostels that Schirrmann had established were school classrooms, converted to provide temporary accommodation while otherwise closed for the holiday seasons. By 1912, however, the first permanent youth hostel (still in operation today) was established in the newly renovated Altena Castle in the German province of Westphalia and, by 1931, a network of some 2,600 hostels existed throughout Europe.

Schirrmann's radical concept became the origin of the International Youth Hostel Federation, now known as Hostelling International, which today oversees the operation of over 3,000 hostels around the world. Travel guidebooks often refer to the hostels in this network as 'official' hostels, but there are now many other hostel franchises as well as countless other 'unofficial' hostels, independently owned and operated, and completely unaffiliated with any centralized organization.

Today the proliferation of both official and independent hostels has helped to create a worldwide culture of backpackers and globetrotters of all ages, backgrounds and nationalities.

This is surely a profoundly positive social phenomenon. In a celebrated editorial in *Time* magazine (16 Dec 2002), columnist Michael Elliot had this to say about it: "The freedom to travel safely and cheaply is one of the great blessings of our time - something that immeasurably expands the range of human experience... Few modern social developments are more significant and less appreciated than the rise of backpacker travel. The tens of thousands of young Australians, Germans, Britons, Americans and others who wander the globe, flitting from Goa to Costa Rica, from Thailand to Tasmania, are building what may be the only example of a truly global community."

Like many Americans, I first became acquainted with the concept of hostelling upon making the post-college pilgrimage across the Atlantic, where I had the good fortune of staying in some excellent hostels in England, Wales and Scotland. As a social extrovert and a committed budget traveler (in other words, *cheap*), I was more than willing to exchange the privacy one gets in a typical hotel room for the shared accommodations of a typical hostel dormitory. In fact, hostels seemed to provide everything I was looking for:

affordable lodging that made possible a wider range of travel, and an inherently social environment that made it *impossible* to sequester oneself from one's fellow human beings.

Unlike many Americans, upon returning to the States, I soon became aware of the fact that hostels exist virtually everywhere. Over the years, in the course of my many travels, I would end up staying in scores of them, in fact, more than I can even remember.

If travel broadens the mind, then I am convinced that hostelling broadens it further. Pablo Picasso once said of his paintings that one of his techniques was to juxtapose starkly different objects within the same canvas and then try to make them all get along. This has always reminded me of our global community in general and hostelling in particular. With so many different kinds of people all sharing the same environment, one never knows exactly what one is going to get, for better or for worse. And yet, 99% of the time, at least in hostels, everyone gets along famously.

My own experiences in this regard have ranged from the sublime to the ridiculous. The best moments in hostelling always seem to center on the instantaneous friendships one makes with others. I once found myself at a hostel in Victoria, Vancouver Island with an atmosphere so warm and congenial that I altered my travel plans in order to stay much longer, only to discover that most of the other guests had done just the same thing. At a hostel just outside of Reykjavik, Iceland, during the dead of winter, the only other guests besides my girlfriend and myself were a chain-smoking couple from Iceland and an archetypal, weathered fisherman from the Faroe Islands. The five of us huddled together in the cold made an intimate, bizarre and happy little family that I shall never forget. On the other hand, at a flophouse of a hostel in San Francisco's Tenderloin district, I encountered the strangest cast of characters I would probably ever meet all in one place: hard-core punks, hopeless drunks, pure eccentrics, certifiable lunatics and drug addicts of every persuasion. That turned out to be a pretty good time as well, and I ended up staying there for over a month.

In any event, I eventually became such a fan of the world of hostelling that it soon became a goal to run a hostel of my own. After all, one can't always afford to travel the world, but running a hostel makes it possible for the world to come to you. For two or three years I kept my eyes out for the perfect opportunity, only to discover that although there might be a lot of hostels in the world, there were also a lot of people who wanted to work in them. It wasn't easy to get a foot in the door.

Nevertheless, after a good deal of patience and perseverance, the perfect opportunity finally presented itself. It was at a hostel that I had stayed at once before and one for which I had a terrific fondness. A management position had opened up and I went after it hook, line and sinker. After finally being offered and accepting the position, I was often asked if I had ever run a hostel before, and my standard line was that I hadn't, but that I *had* done a lot of other unusual things that lent themselves well to such an endeavor. Specifically, I had worked at community centers, homeless shelters and a psychiatric institution. Working at a hostel, I joked, would be the perfect synthesis of all of the above.

On the one hand, I had no idea how accurate this joke would turn out to be. On the other hand, the blessings and the challenges that came with the job also far exceeded anything that I had ever done before. I am grateful for every moment of it.

The hostel is real and the stories are true, although some of the names have been changed in order to protect both the innocent and the guilty. As for the setting, although the astute reader or the savvy traveler can probably discern it quite easily, I will say only that the hostel in this narrative is located on a remote island off the United States, somewhere in the North Atlantic.

Chapter 1

A Cold Windy Island

In which I arrive at my remote island outpost, meet the previous managers and the new crew, and become acquainted with my new surroundings.

The architecture itself was just as I had remembered it, but this time the hostel seemed different. Grand and austere, the building evoked the spirit of a proud seaworthy vessel. Perched as if upon the edge of the world, looking out over the cold, grey Atlantic Ocean, just as it had done for well over a hundred years, the structure of this building was just a marvel to behold. And seeing it like this, alone and amidst the sounds of the seagulls and the crashing waves, it seemed to me for the first time to be almost a living, breathing entity.

I arrived during that nebulous time between winter and spring, which pretty much reflected my own state of mind. I knew that taking a job like this would require a complete overhaul of one's existence. In order to start a new life I had to sacrifice the old one, leaving good friends and loved ones and all that had become comfortable and familiar far behind. But now that I had finally arrived at the setting of my life's next chapter, I had expected a sense of psychological settling in that was still somehow eluding me. The old life was over but the new one had yet to begin.

I had stayed at this hostel before, but now I was returning to take the helm, which seemed an awesome responsibility. Fortunately for me, the previous managers of the hostel, Larissa and Martin, were also there at this time as Martin was putting the finishing touches on some grounds work that he had started at the end of the last season. I took their presence as a godsend. I had had a few days of training a nearby hostel just before I arrived, and there were still a couple of weeks left before we opened for the season, but I certainly felt the need to be walked through the initial process just the same.

Martin came across as your quintessential crusty old sea dog, gruff on the outside but with a heart of gold beneath the surface. Larissa was the personification of sweetness. Together they had the ideal combination of qualities for this line of work. In fact, they had been running hostels for other people for many years, but they had finally just acquired one of their own. I had a lot to learn from them and they had a lot to teach. It was a good situation and I was very glad to have them there.

One of my first responsibilities after being offered the position was to hire a new crew. This wasn't an easy task, primarily because it had to be done long distance and mostly via e-mail. I received many resumes and letters of interest from people who seemed qualified, but who weren't able to commit for the entire length of the season. I also received applications from a number of people who couldn't spell, and from some who couldn't spell the word 'hostel'. In the end I eventually whittled the field down to about four or five applicants, two of whom I would eventually hire.

My decision was based on two factors. First and foremost, I wanted to find people who would be capable and reliable on the job. But I was also looking for people who could demonstrate the strength of character and sense of adventure that would be required for any position that would necessarily involve such a complete change in lifestyle.

Choosing my First Mate was easy. Osman had an impressive resume and had primarily worked in the world of finance. But he seemed determined to take a career sabbatical that would give him a greater sense of meaning and fulfillment in his life, even if it meant an enormous cut in pay. He also seemed like a genuinely interesting and intelligent person, who probably would have been highly qualified for my own job had he been interested in it.

Finding his counterpart was slightly more difficult. If I was going to choose Osman I was encouraged by my off-island supervisors to choose another male, as the two people I would hire would also be sharing the same living quarters. Of the rest of the male candidates, Serge stood out strongly from the rest. His background had been primarily in the restaurant and bar industry, but he had also spent nine months working at one of my favorite hostels in New Orleans.

This particular hostel is a swirling chaotic party scene in the Big Easy, and it's a hell of a place, but quite different from the kind of hostel that I would be running, which aspired to be more, let's just say, *respectable*. In fact, the people who hired me objected to me hiring Serge solely on the basis that he had worked there. I felt that this was unfair. Furthermore, after speaking to a number of Serge's references, and having had a number of telephone conversations with Serge, I chose to hire him over their objections. He definitely seemed like a fun, likable person with an energetic outlook and an enthusiasm for hostelling. He may have been something of a wild card, but he was a risk I was willing to take.

When Osman and Serge eventually arrived, I liked them from the start. Different people with different strengths, they immediately got to work and made themselves incredibly helpful. We all seemed to get along very well, both professionally and personally, which was important. The hiring process had not been easy, but I now felt quite confident that I had made the right decisions. Of course, to be certain, only time would tell.

*　*　*

During those initial days I also took the time to acquaint myself with my new surroundings. This was the first time I had ever lived on an island and I found the environment enchanting. On some days you could smell the salt in the air, and on some days the fog rolled in so thick that you could hardly see ten feet in front of you. On rare occasions it was clear and sunny. On other occasions we received rains of biblical proportions. More often than not, the wind was howling and rattling at the window frames.

The ocean was just close enough that you could see it from the hostel, and the beach itself was just about a three-minute walk away. The waves on this particular end of the island were always enormous. On clear nights, the stars would come out in dazzling multitudes, with the wide swath of the Milky Way cutting right across the night sky. And for some reason the sounds of the waves always seemed much louder at night than they did during the day. But not quite as loud as the frogs! For just beyond the hostel was a large marshy wetland area, and at night it would sound as though there had to have been thousands of them out there, spring peepers peeping away like a deafening chorus.

The first time I went down to the beach the waves were amazing and the sounds they made crashing against the shore were so loud that they roared clearly over the Waterboys' *Fisherman's Blues* recording blaring loudly over my headphones. (I should note that this was during the early aughts when some of us still had portable cassette players with headphones. Just saying.) I sat myself down about ten or fifteen feet away from the water for about a half an hour or so, completely mesmerized and lost in the sea.

I soon realized that I wasn't alone. Off to my left, just a few feet away, I suddenly noticed a small harbor seal was also sitting on the beach. This soon made for a rather sublime experience, just the two of us with the beach all to ourselves, sitting quietly, staring at the waves and subtly regarding each other.

* * *

Those first few days were also among the *last* few days that I had to frolic, as I soon realized just how much work there was to be done. The first task was simply to make the hostel presentable. There were two main hostel buildings. The first one was built in the 1800's, essentially as a coast guard station, originally known as a lifesaving station, and it now housed the women's dorm on the upper level, and the communal kitchen, dining room, living room and front office on the lower level. The back building, which had been built somewhat later, housed the men's dorm on the lower level, and the mixed, co-ed dorm on the upper level.

There were also two smaller staff houses. My little cottage, which I christened *The Pequod*, suited me perfectly, just one large room with a bed, a desk, a table and plenty of bookshelves, plus a small kitchen and bathroom. It was sparse, but I needed nothing more. Martin had just renovated the second staff house for Osman and Serge, which they dubbed *The Endurance*. To be more precise, Martin pretty much rebuilt the thing with his own bare hands and it looked incredible.

In any case, with such a large property containing no less than four historic structures, there would certainly be an overwhelming amount of work ahead just to maintain the place physically. Still, after about a week, with five of us working around the clock, I had to admit that things were starting to look pretty good. And by the time opening day came around, everything had fallen into place and we were finally ready to welcome our first arrivals.

Chapter 2

Opening Day

In which a rowdy college fraternity teaches the lesson that things don't always go according to one's expectations.

In the end, opening day didn't turn out quite as I expected.

We had a single woman booked for the women's dorm and our first big group booked for the men's dorm. The group just so happened to be a fraternity from a highly regarded east coast Ivy League school. But even so, they were still a fraternity, and given our aforementioned standards of 'respectability', it never seemed to me like the wisest choice of bookings. The reservation had been made long before I had come onto the scene.

Ann, our first guest, arrived in the early afternoon. I checked her in, found her to be quite nice, and all was well. Couldn't have been easier! But although the office officially closed at 10pm, our fraternity had planned on catching a late ferry, which meant that they wouldn't arrive until at least an hour later. Earlier that day, we had moved a number of beds from the main building to the back building in order to accommodate them all. And because they would be arriving so late, we even made up their beds ahead of time and made sure that everyone had extra blankets as it was still quite cold at night. During the day I had also washed out all of the barbecue grills outside because I knew that they wanted to use them the following afternoon.

The frat arrived shortly after eleven. I welcomed them to the island and soon met Sam, their contact person with whom I had been dealing over the phone. I took him aside and gave him a written copy of the hostel's policies, all of which had been explained to him already, but I just wanted to make sure that everyone in his fraternity was familiar with them as well. Even though there was only one other guest on this first night, the policies were still in place as guidelines for communal respect. Quiet hours needed to be observed and alcohol was not permitted on hostel grounds. Anyplace else was fine, and we didn't have a curfew, but drinking at the hostel, *per se*, just wasn't condoned. (And generally, for all intents and purposes, what this really meant was that discretion is advised.) Guidelines like these were simply meant to make the hostel feel safe and comfortable for everyone.

I also told Sam that the group needed to be aware of the fact that Larissa and Martin were staying in a private room in the same building in which they were staying. Sam assured me that he understood our policies, that these policies had been communicated to the group, and that they would be especially quiet and respectful of Larissa and Martin. Pleased to hear this, I escorted the group to their dorm.

It was rather late at this point and I was ready to retire for the evening. But for the next hour or so, I couldn't help but notice that a number of our frat boys were wandering in and out of their dorm. And although they probably weren't making enough noise to disturb any of our neighbors, they were definitely making enough noise to keep me awake. At a certain point I decided that I probably needed to check out what was going on and possibly have a word with them, when Larissa suddenly arrived at my door and announced: "We have a big problem!"

Apparently, in direct contradiction to everything that had been said to me, our boys had deliberately snuck in truckloads of alcohol in their suitcases and, unbeknownst to me, had commenced with an enormous, binge-drinking frat party from the moment they first arrived. Initially, Larissa and Martin had been thinking the same thing that I had, which was that maybe they would eventually begin to settle down, but now it was quite clear that the party was only just beginning. And because Larissa and Martin were staying in the same building, they were privy to the details of this party, which included such fraternal activities as group chanting, jumping down stairways, and contests in which our Ivy League brothers felt the need to compare and contrast the size of their 'members'.

Having finally had quite enough, Larissa and Martin marched out of their room, which incidentally startled the fraternity, because Sam *hadn't* actually bothered to tell his brothers that they didn't have the building all to themselves. With bottles and cans all over the place, and at least half of the group underage, they were pretty much caught red-handed. Martin shouted something angry at them, and then he and Larissa stormed out of the building to find me.

I immediately went to confront Sam, who appeared genuinely mortified. I told him that we had extended every possible courtesy to him and his group and that, in exchange, they had completely trashed our policies, which had been explained to them clearly from the start. Moreover, he had overtly lied to me. The entire situation was nothing short of disgraceful. Sheepishly, Sam told me that he was full of remorse and that they would clean up everything right away. Indeed they would, I replied.

And then Sam told me that they wanted to continue their party at the beach first.

Under the circumstances I found this to be a rather astonishing move and I told him that, in fact, they would not be continuing the party at the beach. Instead they would go inside, clean up their mess, turn off the lights and, furthermore, in light of this belligerence, they would have to leave first thing in the morning. This may have been a split-second decision on my part but as far as I was concerned their behavior here was no longer tenable.

Sam then tried to put up a fight. At this point it was becoming personal and I decided I wasn't having any of it. This was my first official night as the manager of this hostel and I was being forced into the unfortunate position of playing babysitter. I felt I had no choice but to raise my voice and restate my demands. Finally they acquiesced and returned to their dorm.

Moments later they were outside again, determined to keep the party going in spite of everything. By this time Osman had woken up and had come to my aid. Together we confronted the group and tried to get them to cooperate with us and demonstrate a modicum of honor and respect. Once again, I reminded them that they were in violation of our policies, that at least half of them were drinking underage, and that if they didn't cut the bullshit, once and for all, I would have no choice but to call the police. Once again they agreed and went back inside.

And moments later they were at it again. And once more we repeated the whole scenario. And then we did it again. Finally it became quite clear that, left to their own devices, this would continue indefinitely. It was now nearly 3am and we had given them multiple warnings. Osman and I were still standing guard outside their building, discussing our options, when they tried sneaking out once again, this time - cleverly - out the back door. A motion detector light immediately came on and they stopped in their tracks to find us glaring at them.

"Oh shit," muttered one of them.

I went ahead and called the police, which was the last thing I wanted to do. I explained the situation in detail and said that I didn't want to cause a commotion but that I was at my wit's end and didn't know what else to do. The dispatcher told me the police would be right over.

I delivered the news to the fraternity and was met with the response: "Oh well, we've had the cops called on us before."

After about fifteen minutes the police arrived. Unfortunately, they were nicer than Osman and I had been. But they did force the kids to pour out all of their remaining alcohol and threatened them with charges and a night's stay at the jail if they didn't comply. Ultimately they said that it was my call what happened next. I simply restated my earlier demands. They would clean up their mess, go to sleep, and leave the hostel in the morning. We then set the time. If I was to have only three hours of sleep, then so would they. Finally, at the end of a very long ordeal, and only after the police had come to back us up, our guests went back inside, turned out the lights and stayed inside.

In the morning, I marched over to wake them up and was surprised to find them already at work. The scene of the crime had been cleaned up and they were packing their bags. I then called their cabs for them, and shortly thereafter they were a thing of the past.

Opening day had been a rude awakening for me, but there were a few silver linings. For one, I had had to deal with my first difficult problem on the first night of the season and, to be honest, I wasn't entirely certain that I had made all the right judgment calls. As a result, I was all the more gratified that all my colleagues backed me up and agreed that I had done the right thing. Furthermore, the university backed me up by giving the boys a slap on the wrist and charging them with several hours of community service. I also figured that, after this initial trial by fire, things could only get easier. (All downhill from here, I hoped!) And finally, in the aftermath of this incident, we managed to discover twelve unopened bottles of nice craft beer that had somehow escaped the purge. Of legal age and in our own private quarters, we were certainly allowed. And at this point, they were well earned!

Chapter 3

A Dark and Stormy Night

In which a series of scattered strange incidents leads us all to believe that the hostel may be haunted!

A few nights later the fog rolled in again. It was amazing how quickly it could sneak up on you. One minute it would be perfectly clear with a few clouds far off on the horizon, and the next minute the fog would descend upon the island like a blanket. Occasionally it would get so thick that at some point the word 'fog' seemed inadequate. (I would learn later that the Scottish call it the *haar.*) When the fog rolled in at night, the lights outside would turn into well-defined beams, almost like searchlights.

The hostel had emptied out again and it was back to just the five of us. On this particular night, Larissa, Martin, Osman and Serge were hanging out in the main building and I was in the Pequod, having just wrapped up some paperwork. I then decided to head over to join the others, but as I left my cottage I paused for just a second just to take in the view. The architecture of the main building really was breathtaking, and especially at night. And currently, the lights downstairs were all on, illuminating the heavy fog creeping around the building. It was a sight to behold.

Because our main building had originally been built as a lifesaving station overlooking the ocean, it was crested on the top with a structure known as a *cupola* - essentially a lookout tower, almost like a mini lighthouse. From the cupola, the men stationed there in times past could watch for ships that had either wrecked or were in distress, and when their aid was needed they would climb aboard their lifeboats and rush out to sea to rescue endangered sailors.

On the very first day I had arrived at the hostel, Martin and I had replaced a broken light bulb in the cupola and had tried to turn it on, but when we flipped the switch all we got were some rather dangerous sparks. The exterior of the tower had certainly seen better days and the electrical wiring had taken a beating from the constant weathering. At some point we would simply need to replace the fixture.

In any case, standing outside my cottage, pausing for a few seconds just to take in the view, something suddenly changed. Looking up, I saw that the light in the cupola, at the very top of the building, had suddenly come on, dramatically illuminating the misty spaces all around it. It stayed on for about five beats and then it went off again.

This was odd, I thought. My first assumption was that Martin might have been upstairs trying to work on the light, but then I noticed that none of the upstairs lights were on. And without those lights it would have been pitch dark upstairs and well nigh impossible to find one's way into the tower. I felt an eerie feeling and the hairs on the back of my neck rose just a little.

I went inside where I found everyone hanging out in the living room, and I told them what I had just seen. The first thing that Martin exclaimed was, "I told you the place was haunted!"

He had. The story from the previous season had been that one night a woman staying upstairs had woken from her sleep to see a strange man walking around the women's dorm. She nervously screamed at him, telling him that he was in the wrong place when he then just vanished before her eyes. After the same thing happened to her again the next night she decided to check out early, saying that nothing like that had ever happened to her before and that she was too afraid to stick around to find out if it would happen again. She was the only one who had seen anything, but that was the legend according to Martin.

In any case, after everyone's nerves settled a bit, I suggested that a more rational explanation for the light coming on in the cupola might be that the wind may have affected the wiring, briefly triggering it on as a result. Osman mentioned that if this were the case then it could be a potential hazard and suggested that we should remove the light bulb and make sure that the power was off. I thought this was a fair enough idea and asked if anyone wanted to join me.

No one did.

So I marched upstairs with a curious combination of fearlessness and trembling. I groped for the light in the women's dorm, found it, and then climbed up the ladder into the cupola. I opened the trap door and ascended into the dark little room, the wind and the mist howling through the cracks in the windowpanes. Steadily, I reached up for the light bulb, unscrewed it, double-checked the power switch and then went back downstairs. The deed was done.

Tales from a Hostel at the Edge of the World

Later that evening, before heading off to bed, Osman and I were hanging out in the Pequod discussing things that go bump in the night, when I suddenly saw the shadow of a person outside passing outside of my side door, simultaneously accompanied by an unnaturally loud bang on the door, and then the shadow moved on as quickly as it had come. Osman and I were both completely startled by this incident - and especially by the surprising volume of the noise - and we stopped our conversation in mid-sentence.

Our first thought was that, considering the evening's events, Serge might have been playing a practical joke on us, but we soon found him inside the main building on the computer at the front desk. When we told him what had happened he seemed more startled than we were and he came right back with us. Serge then suspected that the prank might have been Martin's doing and he went up to Martin and Larissa's room to check, only to find them fast asleep with all the lights turned off.

Whatever the case, it was almost the witching hour by now and time to retire, which we soon did. As I lay in bed contemplating the night's events, my overactive imagination began to entertain the following possibility: It was a rough night out on the ocean, with little to no visibility for any passing ships, which made for a potentially dangerous situation. Had a former resident from times past wanted the light on in the cupola? Even if ships couldn't be spotted from there, at least they might be able to see the light's beams shining through the heavy fog and the cupola could thus serve as a makeshift beacon. By taking the light bulb out, I might have interfered with this intention, potentially placing lives at risk, and had perhaps made a certain someone terribly angry, possibly angry enough to express a sense of frustration by banging loudly on my door and scaring the bejesus out of me!

It was just a theory. But in the morning I woke up early, went straight up to the cupola, and promptly replaced the fixture. In other news that morning, Larissa reported that she had had a difficult time getting to sleep that night, having thought that she had heard someone outside her window, whistling the same tune repeatedly for nearly an hour.

* * *

Scattered strange incidents continued to occur over the next several days. But the constant occurrence was always the back door of the main building, which was right at the bottom of the stairs leading up to the women's dorm.

It seemed that several times a day I would pass by and notice that it was open and unlocked. I would then pull it shut until it latched tightly, and then later in the day I would find it open again. Initially I thought that it had just been someone else who was opening it when I wasn't around.

That was until the day when I was working in the building all by myself. I had shut the door once and no later than fifteen minutes found it open again. Once again I latched it tight. Perhaps an hour later, most of my work done for the day, I was silently reading a book in the living room. There was still no one else in the house, and this time I clearly heard the door unlatch. This was immediately followed by the sounds of very distinct footsteps walking up the stairs.

Impulsively and almost instinctively, I then chose to do something that I never would have done had anyone else been around. I walked over to the unlatched door, shut it, and announced in a loud and clear voice that I was enchanted by the fact that we seemed to have a presence in the house, but that it was my responsibility to lock the door for the purposes of security. If someone else was planning on opening the door all season, then I would continue to close the door all season, because that was my job. It was just that simple. I added that a spooky little incident here and there was perfectly tolerable, but that if things weren't toned down a little, truth be told, it would really start to freak me out. Most importantly, I also announced that the scaring of any guests would not be tolerated.

After my speech, and for the rest of the season, nothing like this ever happened again and the back door stayed shut.

Chapter 4

Good Times Ahead

In which the season begins in earnest with many delightful characters checking in as guests and checking out as friends.

The season soon picked up and our guests began to arrive in droves, many of whom would check in as strangers and check out as life-long friends. One of our very first guests was a great guy from Germany named Frank. To be more accurate, Frank was almost like a cartoon character posing as a hosteller. Incredibly animated, his eyes would light up as he would regale us with his stories of the day's adventures, in such a great singsong German accent that we couldn't help but laugh with delight when we were around him.

"*To-day*, I went *down* to the *beach*," he would say, annunciating and elongating every vowel in his own extremely funny way, "and I *saw* a *seal, swimming* in the *water*!"

We were all crazy about Frank from the start but when he started buying us pastries and gourmet coffee he totally won our hearts, and it was a bittersweet moment when he would eventually check out. Larissa and Martin soon had to leave as well, but they stuck around long enough to meet Frank and, as Larissa would say later on, it was people like Frank who made hostelling worthwhile.

The island was not only a popular destination for travelers and vacationers but also for lots of kids from all over the world who came to look for seasonal work, and for most of them the hostel was the logical starting point. One day four Dominicans showed up from out of the blue. They arrived without reservations and they entered through the back door, but Fina, Rosi, Ismael, and Arturo quickly became our great friends. They were fun kids with hearts of gold who could always put a smile on your face. We bonded over numerous barbecues and elaborate Dominican dishes that Fina and Rosi would cook up. On a clear night that featured a spectacular lunar eclipse, we lit a fire on the beach to keep us warm, another great guest played the guitar, and Ismael and Arturo introduced us to an excellent

Dominican rum. We spent a magical evening together, singing songs under the stars as we watched the celestial dance unfold.

A few days later, Ismael and Arturo returned to the hostel sometime in the afternoon and told me that the girls had just witnessed a duck getting hit by a car. I really didn't know how to respond to this. "That's too bad," was pretty much all I had. A short while later Osman came around and asked me if I had seen the duck. I told him that I hadn't, but that the boys had told me the story. Osman then informed me that what he was referring to was the dead duck sitting in a plastic bag just outside the hostel! At this point I was hoping for some clarification, but Ismael and Arturo had disappeared again. That night, however, as soon as Fina and Rosi returned, they got straight down to business preparing the evening's meal: fresh duck! They seemed to know what they were doing alright, but I was naturally a little hesitant about the endeavor, what with all the feathers and blood and boiling water going on in the kitchen. Not to mention thoughts of botulism.

I quickly got online and found a site all about cooking birds from scratch, which confirmed that the girls, of course, knew exactly what they were doing. Osman and I then watched them at work in the kitchen, bemused and astonished by their culinary arts. Our Dominican friends, on the other hand, seemed rather bemused and astonished by the simple fact that we didn't know how to cook a duck! A couple hours later we all sat down to a delightful meal.

Being rather maniacal about cleanliness, I made sure that everyone helped to scrub down the kitchen afterwards. There were feathers absolutely everywhere, but after a while it seemed that we had scoured every square inch of the place. If anyone had suspected the existence of an erstwhile duck in our kitchen, there was no trace of it now.

The next day, however, I noticed that there were still a few feathers that had somehow managed to elude us, so I cleaned the place up all over again. Nevertheless, for the rest of the season and up until the final weekend, I would every now and then happen across a small stray feather cleverly concealing itself just beneath a chair or right around a corner.

By the time Raul showed up it was clear that the festival of food had only just begun. Raul was maybe fifty-something, originally from Costa Rica, but raised in Columbia and he came to the island via Florida. He had come to work at one of the higher end restaurants for the season, which was fitting because his passion for cooking was unrivaled. On the rare occasions when he wasn't making us something spectacular to eat, he was talking about eating, about all of the restaurants he had worked in, about the recipes he learned while living and working in Italy, about the overwhelming variety of sauces there were in the world. (Although 'sauces' were always called 'salsas'.) He could go on in this wise for hours, and whenever anyone would stop to ask him why all he ever wanted to talk about was food, his usual reply would be, "Hey, everybody's gotta eat!"

But there was more to Raul than just food. He soon became something of a father figure for the Dominicans and he did everything he could to help them find work and housing - even before he was able to find housing of his own. And he would end up going well out of his way to help out almost everyone else who showed up at the hostel looking for the same things. He was a master at networking, tooling around the island in his little blue car, talking to people and finding out who was looking for workers and who was looking for tenants, and then he'd see to it that everything worked out for everyone. He was a good guy, even if he was a bit obsessive about the food.

Another one of my favorites was Jacob, a funny little guy from Israel with a perpetual smirk on his mouth and a gleam in his eyes, who always had an amusing anecdote to tell. There happened to be a few Israelis staying at the hostel at this time and a group of them, including Jacob, soon found work on a landscaping job. On the first day, according to Jacob, they ended up working with a guy from Texas who apparently hadn't gotten around that much. At one point, Jacob was talking to one of his fellow Israelis in Hebrew and the Texan fellow overheard them.

"What accent is that you're speaking?" he asked them.

They found his question puzzling and told him that they what they were speaking was another language, called Hebrew. The Texan questioned them further and soon learned - apparently for the first time - that people from other countries don't just speak English with different accents, but that they actually speak different languages entirely. His mind was blown by this new information, which almost seemed too much for him to handle. I told Jacob that I found this story to be rather hard to believe and Jacob told me that he did too, but he insisted it was true. Everything happens, I suppose...

Then came the Irish. Dan and Aveen were a young couple from Northern Ireland, with beautiful colorful accents and personalities to match. The first night they stayed with us they had gone out for the evening, and when they came back, after hours, Osman and I were in the Pequod chatting and listening to music over a few beers. Suddenly Dan and Aveen's smiling faces popped up outside my window and we were naturally delighted to invite them in. The evening quickly turned into a good old-fashioned *craic*. We regaled each other with stories and laughter. I put on some traditional Irish music by the Chieftains, which Dan and Aveen found rather a bit too old school, putting on a hilarious impromptu act of an old-fashioned Irish couple romancing each other in the traditional brogue. So instead I put on *Red Roses for Me* by the Pogues and soon we were all singing our hearts out. It was a beautiful evening and we forged a solid bond of friendship over it.

A day or two later, Jimmy showed up from Boston. He had called late at night, wanting to make a reservation right away, and just talking to him over the phone I wasn't at all sure about him. He seemed like trouble. But I didn't have a good reason not to let him in, so he arrived shortly thereafter. He was an older, almost stereotypically Irish American, working class kind of guy. And what a big guy he was - probably weighing in at somewhere around 300 pounds. Another colorful, affable character, he thanked me for letting him stay with us, and presented me with gifts of delicious Italian bread and cheese from Boston's North End.

A kind gesture, to be sure, but I still wasn't sure about him. Something about him just wasn't quite right. Among other things, a red flag went up when he made an issue about how long he had been sober after decades of alcoholism: nearly two months. I was told afterwards that throughout that night he stayed with us, he made periodic visits to the restroom, loudly vomiting into the toilets and disturbing everyone in the building. After talking with him, I believed that he was sober. After hearing about the retching, I believed that he was suffering from serious detoxification effects.

Like Dan and Aveen, Jimmy was also there to look for work and housing, and the three of them eventually got to chatting about it. Jimmy said that he had found a group house that they could all move into right away. Dan was enthusiastic about the alliance, perhaps naïvely so, while Aveen seemed a little bit more guarded and concerned. Nevertheless, a day later they all moved in together.

About a week after that, Dan and Aveen returned to the hostel to tell us their tale of woe. All was not well living under the same roof as Jimmy, and they were visibly disturbed. I took them into the Pequod and had them tell us everything. Apparently Jimmy had become violent and maniacal. Furthermore, he had now taken on a new name for himself: *Boston Powers*!

Tales from a Hostel at the Edge of the World

Each night his behavior became more and more erratic and unpredictable, more and more delusional, and it had boiled to a head the night before, when a violent eruption had them both afraid for their lives. Aveen seemed on the brink of a nervous breakdown. Dan felt responsible for the whole thing.

After hearing their stories I was more convinced than ever that Jimmy was undergoing serious side effects and had become delusional and dangerous as a result. I soon found some information about a crisis center on the island that served as a resource for dire situations like this one, and I had Aveen call their hotline. She explained the situation over the phone and, minutes later, Osman drove them down to the courthouse where they met with a lawyer and a judge and filed a restraining order on Jimmy. And then the police evicted Jimmy from the group house.

Later that night, just as I had feared, Boston Powers himself returned to the hostel hoping to check in. But my story had already been set: We were expecting a large group of girl scouts who had booked the hostel for the whole weekend. He would have to try us again at a later date. Boston Powers meekly accepted the news and then drove off. Fortunately, we never saw him again.

Karen and Donal were from Dublin and, by the time they arrived, somewhat later in the spring, it had become a bit more difficult to find work. They had come with nothing but high hopes about finding work in America, but after weeks of steadfast persistence, their spirits were eroding, their money was running out and they had come to the bitter conclusion that it was probably time to turn tail and head back to Ireland.

I was torn up about this because I was really fond of them both and didn't want to see them leave brokenhearted. We were having one of our ritual Sunday afternoon barbecues when Donal told me the news about their decision. I told him that I understood their frustration but that I had seen others facing the same difficulties and that so far everything had worked out for everyone. I did my best to encourage him to steady on for just a little bit longer, but he would have none of it. With the current state of their finances, he just felt that they could no longer afford to take any more chances.

It seemed that no sooner did he tell me this that I heard my phone ringing and I ran to answer it. Incredibly, it was a woman who lived down the street who was calling to say that she was looking for someone to help her out with some random cleaning, moving and various other odd jobs around her house. She said that it wasn't anything more than a temporary job but that she was willing to pay well and she just wondered if we happened to have anyone staying with us who might be interested. I asked her how soon she wanted someone over there and she said right away. I took her address and phone number and told her that she would have a lovely young couple from Ireland there right away!

I passed the news on to Karen and Donal and their faces lit up. They bounced into action, ran down to the address I gave them and started immediately. The job only lasted about three days, but it helped them to get by financially, and the neighbor who employed them later called me back to tell me just how much she had appreciated their help. They ended up making just enough money to keep at it for a few days more, and by the end of the week they had both found jobs that would keep them on the island for the rest of the season. I was pleased as punch!

Those were just a few of the stellar people who graced our hostel so early into that first season, and we were very fortunate that so many of them would be staying on the island as long as we were. After getting themselves situated with jobs and housing, many of our alumni would often drop by from time to time just to hang out and have a laugh, and the reunion barbecues continued every Sunday. Without a doubt, it was people like these who made hostelling worthwhile.

Chapter 5

Born Again Christians

In which the hostel is plagued by a bundle of contradictions.

As it happened, my decision to hire Serge would turn out to be something of a disaster. At first things seemed fine. Serge wasn't exactly the sharpest knife in the drawer, but he did have a good attitude and his initial mistakes were relatively minor. Nevertheless, I should have seen the signs earlier. After all, on opening night, when the frat boys were giving us such grief, Osman was the first to jump in and help, while Serge was apparently quite content to let us deal with it alone.

Other problems emerged later. On one occasion I overheard Serge take a call from someone who was trying to make reservations at a different hostel. We had the contact information for this hostel on file but rather than giving her the correct number to call, he simply told her, "Sorry sweetheart, we don't take reservations for them here. OK. Bye-bye!" When I asked him afterwards why he didn't help her out by at least giving her the correct number, he laughed it off and told me cheerily that he just wasn't in the mood to be bothered. Furthermore, when he would take reservations for our own hostel he would often be very incomplete about it, making mistakes that could have caused some pretty serious problems had I not caught them in time.

And the problems continued. Usually in the evenings, while Osman and I were bonding and having a laugh in the Pequod, Serge would sequester himself online in the office. Fair enough. That was his prerogative, but one morning I awoke to find that he had left the office door not only unlocked but wide open, giving everyone at the hostel open access to the safe and the cash register.

Moreover, I had previously considered it unnecessary to explicitly tell my staff that the computer in the office shouldn't be used for any, shall we say, 'inappropriate' activities. Nevertheless, I made a point of telling them anyway. And yet even after making this clear, I opened the office one morning only to discover that Serge had, in fact, been surfing porn sites. And

I discovered this only because he hadn't even bothered to close the pages.

Serge did have a thing about the ladies. He was, at the time, juggling about four or five different girlfriends, and he told us that he always maintained open relationships because the alternative just wasn't very realistic. Curiously, one day Serge left a notebook of his open on the desk, in which he had written a note to himself that read, "I am happiest when I am making lots of money, working out, getting good sex, and having a positive relationship with God."

This wasn't necessarily the strangest thing about Serge, but it struck me as a little bit weird. It turned out that Serge was a self-proclaimed born-again Christian, who seemed to have no problems reconciling that element of his life with other, perhaps, less compatible elements. He was the son of a preacher man, and he brought with him to the hostel not one, but three different bibles, which he would later sit around reading, usually while on the clock, and often while watching me work. And that was when he wasn't preparing hour-long lunches for himself, and then dozing off in the living room afterwards. Clearly I had a problem on my hands.

* * *

Meanwhile we were all set to receive our second big group reservation of the season, which just so happened to be a non-denominational conference of born-again Christians who had booked up every single spot in the hostel for three days in a row. But even though they had exclusively reserved every single bed we had, I was never told exactly what their numbers would be. When I asked Sister Henrietta, their contact person, she dreamily replied, "I don't know. We'll just have to see how many the Spirit moves…"

It turned out to be not very many. On the first day, curiously, we didn't have a single soul and we enjoyed having the hostel all to ourselves. On the second day, however, the first batch arrived. I was initially expecting the group to be a roomful of Ned Flanders, so imagine my surprise when what we got instead was a rough-edged group of spiky-haired punks who called themselves Youth Storm! Angry adolescents clad in matching black regalia, they sported t-shirts that informed: 'Even demons believe… and tremble!'

One of the most interesting things about the Christian punks was how hard they tried to impress us with just how rotten they had been before they got cool with Jesus. They had done a lot of drugs and gotten in trouble with

Tales from a Hostel at the Edge of the World

the law. One kid had even spat in his mother's face! (We got to hear allusions to that episode repeatedly.) One could easily tell that they were still deriving a great sense of satisfaction from their former wickedness and the street credibility they believed it granted them. But as they transitioned from their war stories to their current crusade, it became more and more clear that the aforementioned mother-spitter was no more than the ringleader. He was the one that the other kids had looked up to in their previous lives, so when he got cool with Jesus and turned his life around, so did the rest of his crew.

The kids described themselves as being 'hard-core' Christians. And for them being hard-core apparently meant being as in-your-face as they could possibly be about their religious beliefs, which of course boiled down to not much more than the simple notion that if you hadn't accepted Jesus Christ as your personal Lord and Savior then you were going to Hell. As soon as I sized them up I decided that the best course of action was just to minimize contact with them. After all, why throw yourself into a dialogue in which the other party has an Absolute Understanding of Ultimate Truth? Best just to let them be, I thought.

Osman was more curious about the kids than I was, and he tried to probe them about their beliefs but all he kept getting were repeated allusions to the same bible verses and repetitive, fervent and oftentimes angry monologues that seemed increasingly unlikely to end well. Eventually, he loaned them his guitar as a means of escape. One of them took it and proceeded to play the same three chords repeatedly while the others chanted along in prayer until they all broke down in tears.

Serge, on the other hand, loved the kids! The kids, however, seemed completely bewildered by Serge. They were obviously pleased that he was saved, but they couldn't quite understand how he could be a born again Christian and embrace the lifestyle he was describing to them at the same time. As he told me later, they just didn't get it.

As it happened, the next day Serge ended up attending their evangelical conference with them and he reported that it was a profoundly moving experience. He said that he had never seen so many people so motivated to do so much good. (I'm still not exactly sure what they were doing, or whom they were doing it to, but I took his word for it.)

On the third day, more members of the conference actually came to the hostel, and they largely resembled a roomful of Ned Flanders. On the final count, there probably hadn't been more than twenty or thirty of them, which meant that Sister Henrietta had spent the vast majority of their money to reserve empty beds. And I think that that may have been the point. As I listened to their conversations I kept hearing the same phrase being used repeatedly. Whenever they would speak about someone they knew who hadn't yet been 'saved', they would shake their heads and refer to that person as still being, sigh, '…still in the world.'

How sad, I thought. Because their whole approach seemed to be in direct contradiction to what hostelling is all about. Instead of being willing to share their space with other people, our born-again Christians apparently preferred to buy up every spot in the compound to effectively shut others out. How much better, it seemed to me, to embrace the world and the diversity it has to offer. Just one man's opinion, but I'd like to think that Jesus might agree. He didn't exactly divorce himself from 'the world'.

* * *

Meanwhile, the problems with Serge were continuing to mount. He continued to make mistakes, everything from inaccurate reservations, to loafing around on the job, to inappropriate behavior around the guests. I continued to do my best to redirect him, but only to see him make the same mistakes time and time again. After many private conversations with him, and after a lot of soul searching on my part, I came to the inevitable conclusion that it was neither in the best interests of the hostel, nor in my best interests, nor even in Sergio's best interests, for his employment to continue. It was a tough decision to make, but after too many egregious incidents of hopelessly poor judgment, including the latest one in which he had personally insulted a guest, I really felt I had no choice.

Fortunately, we were able to make an amicable break. I gave Serge a good amount of time to find a new job and a new housing situation, and I was even happy to serve as a reference for one of his job leads. (Of course, that was mostly just to get rid of him!) In time, everything came together for him and I was glad that we were able to part on decent terms. Serge had been yet another trial for me, but in the final analysis it seemed that everything had worked out for the best, for everyone concerned.

Raul was still staying with us at the time and when he got word of the job opening, much to my surprise, he volunteered for it right away. The day shift hours coordinated neatly with his restaurant job and I could think of no good reason not to bring him on board. He started immediately and on his nights off we ate like kings.

Chapter 6

The Mystifying Oracle

In which two strange mediums arrive at the hostel and we attempt to make contact with Spirits from the Other Side.

Although all paranormal activity at the hostel had ceased after my previous speech at the back doorway, I had felt inclined to make contact with our ghost, assuming that we still had one. I wanted to find out whatever I could. I had shared a few of my stories with friends, some of whom were extremely skeptical and some of whom were quite intrigued. My own perspective was somewhere in the middle. I certainly agree with Shakespeare that there are greater things in the heavens and the earth that are dreamt of in our philosophies. Then again, as they say, everyone should have an open mind, but not so open that one's brains fall out. As far as I'm concerned, the best way to increase our understanding about anything is to be open and skeptical at the same time.

And it was with this perspective that I approached the arrival of the Ouija board that some friends had brought to me after they heard my ghost stories. For the uninitiated, the Ouija board is a phenomenon that sprang from the spiritualist movement of the nineteenth century. Originally known as 'the talking board', it first emerged sometime in the 1880's, consisting of a single board on which were written the words, *yes* and *no*, the letters of the alphabet, the numbers from zero through nine, and, on the very bottom, the word *goodbye*. The idea is that two or more players gather together and lightly rest their fingers on a small heart-shaped platform, known as the *planchette*, which rests upon the board. The theory is that provided the participants have the right mental attitude, the planchette will soon begin to glide across the board, seemingly by its own accord, but utilizing the physical energies of the players, to use the written symbols to spell out messages, which may or may not be communicated from the Other Side.

I had had my fair share of experiences playing around with Ouija boards in high school and college and, naturally, I had witnessed some remarkable things and some less-than-remarkable things. You just never know what you're going to get. Nevertheless, at the very least, having the board at the hostel provided the potential for an experiment, as well as good fun. It was certainly worth a go.

At the very beginning of the season, Osman and I had met three fantastic women who worked at one of the inns in town, and they soon became our fast and constant friends. Jackie was from Scotland, Sarah was from Australia, and Dallice was from New Zealand. All three were great fun and we always enjoyed hanging out together whenever we got the chance. As soon as we told them about the Ouija board they were eager to come over and give it a try.

Interestingly enough, just before moving to the island at the start of the season, our three friends had independently visited psychic readers, each of them for the first time. Although none of them had necessarily placed a whole lot of stock into what they had been told, Sarah's psychic reader in Australia had sensed that she was definitely 'in tune' with the other side. She was told that she had a gift, perhaps one that ran in the family. This might sound rather predictable, but as it happened Sarah's grandmother was a gypsy, of pure Roma stock, and her grandmother had told her the same thing when she was a child.

We initially tried the board with various combinations of us taking turns, to mixed results. But the first time that Sarah and I tried it together, the planchette took off immediately, moving quickly and clearly from letter to letter. This was a breakthrough.

I asked if there was a presence that wished to communicate with us and the answer was *yes*. The purported entity on the other end soon told us that his name was Malcolm Nathaniel, that he had been born on the island in 1838 and that he had died in 1879. His father's name was Malcolm as well and his mother's name was Louise. I went on to ask him if he now lived here at the hostel, and he said that he did! He went on to mention a friend of his by the name of Abe Willetson. I inquired if Abe was there now and he said no, that Abe had moved on. I then asked Malcolm if he wanted to move on himself, and he said *yes*. I asked if he felt that he was able to and he said *no*. I asked if he knew why he couldn't and he said that he didn't. He was stuck here, he told us. There was nothing he could do about it, and there was nothing we could do about it. End of story. At that point, the planchette moved off the board, thus ending the session.

Tales from a Hostel at the Edge of the World

I felt extremely sorry for Malcolm and said as much. At the same time I was ecstatic! I was thrilled that we had not only made contact, but that we had also gotten some extremely specific information.

Now what I wanted was verification. I started online, which yielded some leads for checking birth and death records on the island, as well as a few resources in the way of historical and genealogical organizations. In the next couple of days, I checked out everything I could find, but even after visiting the office of the town records, I came up with absolutely nothing. No corroboration whatsoever. This was a little disheartening. Absence of evidence may not have been evidence of absence, but a little evidence could have gone a long way.

Nevertheless, Sarah and I weren't ready to give up. We got together often to play on the board and the stories not only flowed, but they continued to get richer and richer. Surprisingly, we never heard from Malcolm again, but we did hear from several others. We heard stories of ships and shipwrecks; stories of adultery and treachery; stories of death and murder; stories of tragedy and comedy; stories about men, women and children from all over the world, all of whom somehow ended up on this remote island in the Atlantic, and all of whom somehow ended up as lost souls. Sarah and I were having a blast!

* * *

Jeria was a late arrival. Osman told me that she had called to say that she was on the last ferry to the island, which meant that I would have to wait up for her after the office had officially closed. This wasn't unusual and I was always happy to do what I could to accommodate our guests. After all, that's what we were there for.

Jeria, however, was a rather unusual soul. She had been born in Nigeria but had been spending the better part of the last few years in a religious community somewhere in Brazil. It wasn't quite clear what kind of a religious community she was a part of, but she exuded a quiet and peaceful sense of spirituality. There was something nice and open about her face, and she wore a long flowing white dress along with a matching white cap that covered her hair. She checked in for a week and she was a serene and welcome presence in the hostel. Osman and I both took a liking to her.

Jeff Becan

One day I was talking with Osman at the front desk, and we happened to be discussing a Ouija board session that had occurred the night before. Jeria overheard us and she started asking us questions. Now normally we probably wouldn't advertise to our guests that we believed that the hostel might be haunted and that we regularly played around with a Ouija board in an attempt to communicate with spirits from the other side. (Some people might think that was a little bit strange.) But Jeria was very inquisitive and intrigued and we ended up giving her all the background and including her in the conversation.

After a while, Jeria opened up and confided to us that she felt that she had been guided by spirits to our island, and to this hostel, for a reason. She said that she had the sense that the building itself had been built for the purposes of saving lives and that a life-nurturing essence emanated from it still. She believed that it attracted those who had passed over, but who had not yet passed on, deceased souls who were still clinging onto life, for one reason or another. She then told us that she had never played with a Ouija board before but that she would like to try it with us.

This was all far too strange and unusual to pass up, so we planned for a séance that evening. Jeria and I would be on the board and Osman and Dallice would be the transcribers. I felt certain that Jeria had the right sort of disposition that would make for an excellent medium. And yet, after several attempts, we got nothing. The planchette simply didn't move for us. This certainly wasn't unprecedented but I was still rather surprised. We then tried different combinations of us on the board but nothing was forthcoming. Eventually we decided to give up. Osman and Dallice soon took off for the evening but Jeria stayed for a while to chat.

As the two of us were talking, suddenly Jeria's disposition changed. She had a strange look in her eyes and she said that she felt that something was coming on. I asked her what she meant by this and she said that she felt as if a spirit were trying to communicate through her.

"Have you ever felt anything like this before?" I asked her.

"Never," she replied, "but I want to let this spirit through anyway. I will try."

I wasn't quite sure how I felt about this.

Jeria's eyes rolled back into her head, which she then started rolling around in odd circular motions. Soon she began to speak in a strange, prolonged sort of manner.

Tales from a Hostel at the Edge of the World

"I am... the Lady... Lanora! What is it... you... *seek* from me?" she hissed.

OK, this was a bit strange, even for me. But I decided to roll with it. I calmly told her that I sought information about spirits who might be dwelling at the hostel.

"What *sort* of information... do you *seek*?" she asked.

Well, you know, names, stories, that sort of thing. But also, I wanted to know if there was anything we could do to help any of these spirits move on.

"You are *asking*... the wrong *questions*," was her reply.

Well what sort of questions was I supposed to be asking?

"You know... the *questions*... you should be *asking*. Ask the right... *questions!*"

Lady Lanora wasn't being very helpful. And she was kind of freaking me out. Before drifting into this trance, Jeria had told me that nothing like this had ever happened to her before, and I was beginning to wonder if Jeria would ever return or if we were stuck with the Lady Lanora from here on out. I tried to engage her a little bit more, but she continued to be vague and weird and unhelpful. Finally, I decided to ask her to go away and let Jeria return. It took a little cajoling but eventually her head swirled around a few times and then dropped down dramatically, her eyes closed.

After a couple of seconds, Jeria raised her head again.

"What happened?" she asked, as though she had no idea...

I told her everything that had happened and that no useful information had come through. I also told her that I was glad to have her back and that the whole thing had been rather bizarre.

Jeria was really disappointed. She had hoped that she had been brought to the hostel for a reason and that by serving as the medium for this strange, so-called Lady Lanora, she might be able to help the spirits. But such was not the case. "I feel like a failure," she told me dejectedly. I tried to reassure her that there was no reason to feel bad and that everything would be just fine. Mostly I was just glad to have her back. Nevertheless, she soon left for the evening, with her head hung low, and we never talked about it again.

Later, however, I did ask her some questions about her community in Brazil and she told me a little bit about it. I ended up doing a quick search and discovered that she was part of a strange, new-age cult, led by a guru who regularly went into trances, just like she had done, and who claimed that the spirits spoke through him to deliver transcendental wisdom to his followers.

*　　*　　*

Afterwards, I told the whole story to Sarah and we both had a good laugh about it! She and I continued to have fascinating sessions with the Ouija board throughout the rest of the season. Fantastic stories kept coming through, and we kept on trying to search for corroborating evidence. We never found a scrap. In the end we both concluded that there was nothing that had come through on the board that couldn't simply be coming from our own subconscious imaginations. No ghosts or spirits or other bizarre theories were really necessary. Oh well. It was still a fun little parlor game and, if nothing else, it kept us entertained from time to time.

On one occasion, after coming to our conclusion, we thought it would be interesting to see what would happen if we just told the board that we no longer actually believed in any of the stories coming through.

The response was simply this: "Real life can't be explained here, but behind all messages lies some truth."

Chapter 7

Bad Eggs

In which trouble has a way of finding the hostel and is dealt with swiftly and accordingly.

By and large, there aren't too many factors that would disqualify someone from staying at a youth hostel. In fact, the term 'youth hostel' itself is rather obsolete, but somehow it still lingers. Most hostels around the world are open to anyone regardless of age, race, sex, creed, background, blah, blah, blah, with a few common exceptions. One is that many hostels have policies against housing people who are from the immediate vicinity, a rule of thumb that seeks to prevent the transformation from hostel into flophouse, although those exist too.

But regardless of the openness of the world of hostelling, there are some fairly obvious factors that would make a person unsuitable. You can't necessarily codify these rules, but you know them when you see them. One good guideline is to prevent people from the hostel whom you yourself wouldn't feel comfortable sleeping next to. But this one is tricky too. First, it's subjective. Secondly, it's based on suspicion. And how can one, in good conscience, hold someone guilty until proven innocent?

So the reality is that in many cases you simply have to accept people from whom you might anticipate problems, wait for the problems occur, and then deal with them. Normally, the people who are going to cause problems are obvious from a mile away. Much of the time you can tell who the troublemakers might be just from talking to them over the phone.

Todd was a perfect example. He had called to make reservations. Actually it was more like he had called pleading for reservations. He said that he had never stayed at a hostel before but that he was going through a rough time, something about a divorce, and that he desperately needed a place to stay. I told him that it wouldn't be a problem and that he didn't need to tell me his life's story. All he needed to do was to give me the relevant information and I would put him down in the reservation book. (And by the way, back then, we did have an actual book. We would write the reservation details down in pencil so we could erase them in the event of cancellations. The system worked just as well, if not better, than any reservations software I've used since. Just saying.)

When Todd arrived late at night a few days later, Osman was working the desk, and somehow Todd managed to slip through the cracks. He told Osman that he didn't have any cash to pay for that night but that he would get up first thing in the morning, go to an ATM in town, and bring us the money by 10am. Osman asked him for a credit card instead, but he wouldn't hand any over. However, not only did he indeed have numerous credit cards at the time, but he also had numerous addresses. There was the one he gave me when I took his reservation, there was the one he put in the book when he signed in, and then there were at least three different addresses I found on his luggage tags later. All very suspicious, to say the least.

So he ended up staying for free the first night, but after I heard about his story I confronted him in the morning. He told me again, ever so sincerely, that he was going through a rough time, this time it was a separation. He also told me that 'this guy' owed him money. He was going to go find the guy, get his money, and then come back by noon to pay us. I told him that he really needed to do this or he couldn't stay with us another night. I wrote this out on a piece of paper in the form of an IOU and told him that he had to come back and pay us no later than noon.

Noon rolled around, then one, then two. Finally I went to collect his stuff to have it ready for him to pick up, whenever he might decide to return. All his belongings were on his bed, everything packed neatly in his bags, all except for one item that he seemed to have deliberately set aside for display - a set of motivational tapes with a title that said something about recovering one's lost innocence. That was it, I thought, this guy's a would-be scam artist and he's out of here no matter what.

Another hour or two rolled by and I was getting impatient. The only number I had for him was the number he had given me when I took his reservation, so I called it. I got an answering machine and began to leave a message. "Hello, this is Jeff from the hostel. I'm looking for Todd, who stayed with us last night. He told me that he was going to pay me by this afternoon, but I haven't seen him and I…" At that point someone picked up the phone. "The guy's a bum," the voice on the other end told me. "Kick him out! He's a con artist. He stayed with me for two weeks and he kept promising he was going to pay me and he never did. Throw the bum out!"

Tales from a Hostel at the Edge of the World

Eventually, a truck pulled up with Todd in it. Apparently he had managed to con someone into giving him a ride. By now it was around 5pm. I went out to meet him and told him that he'd better hold onto his ride, because he was no longer welcome at the hostel. I told him that we had had an agreement that he didn't honor, and I also told him that I had called the number that he himself had given me, that the guy on the other end told me he was a con man and that, frankly, I had suspected as much.

"A con man?" he replied, feigning bewilderment, "He said that? I can't believe it… I was coming here to pay you. Do you want me to pay you for last night?" I told him that I did, I wanted him to pay me for the night he slept here and then to move on. "How much do I owe you?" he asked. The answer was $23.00. He pulled out a fat wad of bills from his pocket and counted out the money and handed it to me. I just put it in my pocket and stood over him until he gathered his stuff, which took an extraordinarily long amount of time. "A con man…" he kept mumbling to himself, astonished.

Finally, he left. The guy who had given him the ride had already left. Quite sensibly, he no longer wanted anything to do with the man. So I watched Todd walk down the street, carrying his luggage with him. In fact, I even went up to the cupola for a better view, to make sure that he kept on walking. After I felt certain that he was gone, I pulled the money out of my pocket to ring into the register: $22.00. Only a dollar missing - but still a nice touch!

A few days later I was looking through the local paper, where they actually named names in the police blotter. Sure enough, Todd's name was right there! He was being arraigned for theft and forgery of $200,000. That's what had brought him to the island and that's what had brought him to the hostel. We found out later, because the island is so small, that he had stolen the money from a local woman he had been dating at the time.

* * *

I had a bad feeling about Dean from the moment the phone rang. Before I was even able to get the receiver up to my ear he was already talking a mile a minute. He was calling from another hostel and he wanted to know if we had availability at our hostel that night because he was about to get on a plane to come over and he didn't have a place to stay. All of this information was very rapidly rambled at me.

"How do I get to the hostel from the airport?" he asked.

"Well, you can just catch a… "

"How do I get to town from the hostel?" he continued.

He then proceeded accordingly for about five or six more questions. "OK," he concluded at the end of his conversation with himself, "I'm on my way."

After this extremely bizarre exchange, I concluded (or perhaps just hoped) that we might not even see the guy. But we did. And he was far crazier in person than I had imagined. And by crazy I mean probably strung out on acid. Osman had just checked him in, and I had been sitting in my private cottage reading a book, when my door suddenly flew open and Dean waltzed in, throwing his bags against the wall.

"Hey," he began, staring pointedly at the ceiling, "where's the pizza place?"

"Excuse me," I responded, "but do you think this is the men's dorm? This is actually a private residence and the men's dorm is in the back. Do you want me to show you to the men's dorm?"

"Oh, sorry, man, sorry. I didn't know," he replied. "I'm Dean. Sorry about that, man. Hey, I'm Dean. Nice to meet you. Do you know where the pizza place is?"

"Let me take you to the men's dorm," I answered.

And so I did. Along the way, we started to talk about the pizza place. I asked him if he had a particular place in mind or if he just wanted any pizza place. He told me he was hungry and that he wanted to go to a grocery store. I started to tell him where to find the store, and he started asking me about the pizza place. Then he said that he wanted to go to a club. "Are there any good clubs? Where are the clubs? I want to go to a club." I told him all the clubs were in town. "How do I get into town?" I told him that he could either walk or take a cab. "I don't want to walk." I told him I'd call him a cab.

When the cab came ten minutes later, Dean was busy accosting Osman with bizarre questions about his racial background. Osman couldn't get a word in edgewise, and the cab sat there waiting for Dean to finish his rambling. Eventually we convinced him to get into the cab and off he rode into town.

My assessment at this point was that he was clearly on drugs and out of his mind, but at least he didn't seem dangerous. If he were to go off into town to get something to eat, and maybe even to go to a club, then maybe, just maybe, he might get everything out of his system, get back, sleep it off and then I'd probably get rid of him in the morning. Then again, maybe it wouldn't go quite so smoothly.

Hours later, Osman and I were in the Pequod entertaining a couple of guests. One of them had asked me to tell her some good stories from the hostel. I told her that I had had my fair share of stories but that one of them was currently in the process of playing out. I gave her the setup and told her that I was waiting for Dean to come back to see if he was a problem that needed to be dealt with swiftly, or if he was a problem that could be dealt with in the morning.

Moments later, Dean returned and we saw him go up to the main building, try the door, which was locked at this hour, and then he headed straight for the Pequod and barged through my door once again. "Hey, I'm Dean," he announced to everyone. Hours after our first encounter, his stare remained fixed on the ceiling. "Hey is the hostel closed? I'm hungry. Can I get into the kitchen?" I told him that the building was closed, that he couldn't get into the kitchen until the morning. "That sucks man. Hey, do you have a knife in here? Alright, I'm going to bed. See ya."

We then watched him go back to the main building, try the locked door again, and then return to the Pequod. "Hey, do you have a knife? I've got a knife. And I'm gonna need it too. Just to warn you, these guys are out to get me and they might get here soon. If they come, I'm gonna kill 'em. Just to warn you. OK, I'm going to bed now. See ya." He left, this time for the proper dorm, talking to himself the entire time.

As far as I was concerned, the problem was already solved. Before the talk about killing people he was a major problem, but still something of a question mark. After the talk about killing people he was a danger to others and he needed to be removed immediately.

The police arrived in about ten minutes. There were four of them. I had explained the whole situation over the phone and I explained it to them again when they arrived. They asked for a physical description, and then they scoped out the back building like a swat team, looking for exits from which he might try to flee. After they got the lay of the land they entered the building, found him, and asked him to step outside where they proceeded to ask him some questions. His performance started out well enough, and for a moment I was afraid that he might be able to fake his way out of it. But he didn't. It quickly became clear to them that Dean didn't really know where he was or what was going on. He did, however, know who he was: He was Dean.

In the meantime, I continued to give the police my perspective and they also heard the testimonies of the other guys in the men's dorm, who said that they weren't planning on even closing their eyes with someone like that in the room.

Minutes later, Dean was being handcuffed and taken into the police car. On the way, he stared at me pointedly. "Hey thanks, man!" he shouted. "Thanks a lot!"

I just smiled and waved. The decision had been clear-cut, which had made it extremely easy. In fact, I had to admit, it was even rather enjoyable at this point. This was something that had to be done, and so it was done. All I did was facilitate it. After all, Dean had warned me that there would be people out to get him. All I did was call them.

* * *

About a month had passed since the incident with Dean and everything had been running perfectly smoothly. Too smoothly, I thought. It had been a while since we had had to deal with trouble and I knew something was coming. We were due.

Sure enough, that evening I received two calls and I had a strange feeling about both of them. The first suspect showed up early and he turned out to be perfectly harmless, just a social misfit and an amusing one at that. Michael, my second suspect, hadn't shown up at all and it was already closing time. So I closed the office and proceeded to lock up the building.

That was when the cab pulled up. A shadowy figure soon emerged and ambled towards the door. As Michael met me at the door, the cab pulled off and drove away.

"Oh man," he said, "Where's the cab going?"

"What do you mean?" I asked, "Did you want it to wait for you?"

"Yeah, I have to go into town to pick up my bags."

"Why do you have to pick up your bags? Why didn't you just bring them with you? And why are you getting here so late?"

"Look," he said, "the reason why I'm late is because I had to pick up my bags at the ferry terminal at 10pm." "But it's after ten now. And that means that the office is closed."

"I got here at one minute before ten," he responded, looking at his watch.

"Actually it's well past ten right now and I still don't know why you have to go pick up your bags. Did you plan on coming here from town, checking in, and then going back into town to collect your bags?"

"Yeah, I left my bags at this other place. I had a couple of beers there. They said they would hold my bags for me. It was a bar. I can't remember the name of the place."

"This doesn't make any sense to me. Are your bags at the ferry terminal or at they at the bar?"

"Dude, here's the deal. I had my wallet stolen in Chicago, and I'm going though a divorce right now. I'm having a rough time, and I just need a place to stay."

"Are you coming here from Chicago?"

"No, I'm from Denver. I flew here from Denver."

"Then how did you get your wallet stolen in Chicago?"

"I changed planes in Chicago and my wallet was stolen at the airport."

"I see. So I suppose you don't have any money and you want to stay here for free."

"No, that's not true. I have money. How much is to stay here anyway?"

"Tonight the rate is $25.00."

"Well, there goes my last $25.00."

"So if you only have $25.00, then what are you going to do? If you have to collect your bags from town, you'll need to take a cab. At this point, I'm thinking that I should just call you a cab, you should go into town and get your bags and then find someplace to stay down there. I can give you the names of some inns."

"Look, I'm gonna tell you the truth. I just need a place to stay for the next three nights."

"Well, as I told you over the phone, we only have availability for tonight. The next two nights are fully booked. And I have to be honest with you: I'm not sure I feel comfortable letting you stay here tonight. You come here after we've closed, you reek of alcohol, and your story doesn't make any sense to me."

"Listen, I'm totally sober."

"You reek of alcohol and you just told me that you came from the bar."

"Yeah, I had a few drinks, but I'm totally sober right now. Look man, I really need a place to stay for the next three nights."

"Like I just said, we don't have space for you for the next three nights."

"Dude, I'm gonna tell you the truth: I just spent the day in jail. I was out on the docks and I don't know what was going on. There was this Brazilian girl and she said it was a private dock or something like that and I didn't know it. So the next thing I know the police have me in handcuffs and they arrest me for trespassing. They dragged me out in front of all the tourists like I was John Gotti or something. So I just spent the day in jail and now I have to stay here for the next three nights so that I can go to court on Monday. Here, I'll prove it to you…"

At this point Michael took out a folded piece of paper from his pocket and handed it to me. Sure enough, it was official documentation proving that he had been arrested for trespassing and released from jail earlier that day. I don't know why he thought this was going to help his case.

"Michael, none of this is adding up for me right now. First you tell me that your bags are at the ferry terminal, then you tell me that they're at some bar where you were drinking. You tell me that you're sober which is obviously not the case. Now you tell me that you've just been released from jail. I don't understand where your stolen wallet or your divorce comes into any of this, and I still don't understand why you came here and didn't bring your bags with you."

"Dude, every word that I've told you is true."

"Well, I'm sorry but it's just not adding up to me."

Michael paused for a moment and then answered defiantly, "Well it's not adding up to me either!"

I had to suppress my laughter at this moment. "Michael, here's the deal. I'm going to call you a cab so that you can go into town and get your bags. Now it's my turn to tell you the truth: I'm not comfortable with letting you stay here. As the hostel manager I have to look out for the safety and well-being of the guests here. It's different than a hotel where everyone has a private room. If you were to stay here you'd be sleeping in a dorm room with other guests and the fact is that I don't trust you enough to let that happen. I'm sorry."

Tales from a Hostel at the Edge of the World

Michael continued to plead his case. He showed me the contents of his wallet, which he apparently had on him after all, and which contained $50.00. He tried to tell me that he couldn't understand everything that was happening to him, that he was a graduate from Harvard and that because he was an intelligent guy I should let him stay. I was kind but firm, and in the end Michael ended up accepting his fate. I called him a cab and then we waited another ten minutes for it to show up.

As soon as the cab had been called, the modality of our conversation suddenly shifted. At that point Michael started to confide random details about his life that continued to make little sense. In any case, he seemed oddly at ease. Eventually, the cab pulled up.

"Well," said Michael, shaking my hand, "you've done everything you can."

"I suppose I have," I answered. "I hope you get your life together and get things straight."

"Thanks. Listen, I'm going to tell you the truth: I'm going to end up sleeping in the bushes tonight. Is there any way you can just give me a couple of blankets?"

"Michael, just get in the cab."

Michael got in the cab and rode off into the darkness.

I happened to know this particular cab driver and a couple of weeks later she independently brought up the incident. She told me that as soon as Michael had gotten in the cab he had told her that he was in trouble, that he didn't have any money, and that he wouldn't be able to pay her. Rather than make a big scene about it she just decided that she would drop him off in town without charging him and just be done with it. Michael was very grateful and he asked her if she could make a quick stop at a convenience store along the way. For some reason, she acquiesced. He ran in and soon emerged with a bottle of wine which he presented to her as a token of gratitude! Why he didn't just pay her instead is anybody's guess.

Fortunately, shady characters like these were the exception rather than the norm. And although such incidents were somewhat regular during that first season, in subsequent seasons they almost disappeared entirely. I liked to speculate that word had gotten out amongst the shady underground community that this year this hostel wouldn't be taking any more shit!

Chapter 8

A Day in the Life

In which an exceptional day of craziness is chronicled around the clock.

At the height of the season, with the tremendous traffic we received at the hostel, most days were generally characterized by madness from beginning to end and around the clock. But I knew in my gut that one midsummer day in particular was going to be crazier than all the others. So I decided to document it scrupulously.

    1:45am. Raul talks too much. Ismael used to tell him that to his face but I usually don't. Nevertheless, I've been listening to him ramble on for far too long after he said he was going to let me sleep about twenty minutes ago. Osman, Raul and I had been up late having a few beers and marveling outside at the moon and the planet Mars, and it had seemed like the party had come to a close. Osman had gone off to bed a little while ago, Raul had said he was going to leave, but now he's delivering an absurd monologue about his pseudo-religious beliefs, which include the notion that God sank the Titanic, disbanded the Beatles, shot John Lennon, and paralyzed Christopher Reeve. "Well, Raul," I interjected as soon as I got a chance, "everybody has to believe in something, and I believe that I'll be going to bed now." This finally did the trick and I collapsed upon my bed, knowing full well that the most challenging day of the season was waiting for me in the morning.

    4:45am. The fire alarm is going off. This hasn't happened in months. At the beginning of the season, when the weather was colder, the steam in the men's showers would often set off the alarm, but who would be taking a shower at this hour? My body instinctively jumps up, scrambles for the keys, and runs into the main building to check the panel and disable the alarm. I then inspect the buildings, find no cause of fire, and reassure everyone that it's a false alarm and that we can all go back to sleep. "Please accept my sincerest apologies. I have no idea what could have caused this." We all go back to bed.

Jeff Becan

5:15am. The fire alarm goes off again to the accompaniment of my fiercest expletives. Returning to the alarm panel, I find that the trouble actually seems to be located in the women's dorm. This hasn't happened before. I call upstairs to ask if it's alright if I come up to inspect and twenty-one women give me their consent. Collectively we find no cause. No fire. No smoke. Nothing. After scratching our heads for five or ten minutes, I tell them that I will stand by to monitor the monitor in case it goes off again but that I don't know what else can be done. I stand by the alarm panel for ten or fifteen minutes and then give up and go back to sleep. Fortunately, it doesn't go off again.

7am. My own alarm clock wakes me up from my brief, deep sleep and it's time to tackle the big day. Here's the set-up: For most of June, July and August we've been swamped with large groups of camp kids: YMCA Camps, Girl Scouts, biking groups, etc. Today is the last day of our summer camp phase. However, according to all of my records, one particular camp group was scheduled to arrive on August 4th. So when we got the call from their contact person wanting to confirm their reservation for August 14th, I was at a loss. August 14th was already completely booked. We had certainly been overbooked before. In fact, we seemed to excel at it, but not by as many as twelve people!

It turns out that a few weeks ago this particular camp's contact person had e-mailed my off-island supervisors to ask if she could change their reservation from the 4th to the 14th. For some inexplicable reason, said supervisors had told them that they could do this, but no one had bothered telling me about it. So that was the big challenge of the day. To deal with it, Osman and I had decided that we would convert our staff houses, the Pequod and the Endurance, into makeshift dorm rooms and that we would just find someplace else to sleep for the night. We had originally planned on going camping in the woods behind the hostel, but after the fire alarm incident I realized that I couldn't stray that far from the main building. I wasn't sure where I was going to sleep now, but I would deal with that later.

7:45am. A shower, a cup of coffee and a powerbar later, I open up the office early. The guests are exceptionally needy this morning, the phone is exceptionally busy, and I'm trying to put all of the arrangements into place. It's a busy morning at the desk, but probably not much busier than most mornings. In any case, I love my job.

Tales from a Hostel at the Edge of the World

9:35am. A service woman has unexpectedly arrived to attend to our public access computer, which hasn't been working properly for several weeks. She does something to reprogram the whole system and she's finished after about a half an hour.

10am. Technically all of our guests are supposed to check out of the hostel from 10am until 4pm. This is the time that we take to get all of our cleaning and maintenance done, and there's always a lot to do. Today most of the guests have checked out on time, but they'll be back.

From 10am until around noon Raul does the basic cleaning while I inventory the rooms. Today I figure out that I only have to move one spare bed from the back building into the women's dorm and one spare mattress into the Pequod. We'll have twenty-five women in the women's dorm, which is supposed to sleep twenty-three. The men's dorm and the co-ed dorm will be at full capacity at thirteen beds each. I'll move the four men from the O'Shea family into the Pequod, and we'll have the six camp girls move into the Endurance. Rivaling the miracle of the loaves and the fishes, we somehow not only have enough beds for everyone, but we also have enough pillows.

The Pequod and the Endurance still need to be prepared and I've got four or five loads of laundry to do. In the meantime, our German couple has returned to get their camera from the office, the Billows family has to be chased out of the back dorm so that Raul can clean it, and the O'Shea clan return to sit outside in the sun, staring longingly inside. I still haven't decided where I'm going to sleep.

12:30pm. The new camp group has arrived. Apparently they weren't aware that check-in time is at 4pm. Fortunately, the men's dorm is already done so I can get the boys situated, but Osman still hasn't prepared the Endurance, so the girls will have to wait. In the meantime I get everyone settled in as best as I can and I give them the standard introduction to the world of hostelling. It's all about *respect*, I tell them. Clean up after yourselves, mind the quiet hours, and recognize that you don't have the place all to yourselves. We've got all kinds of different people here from many different countries and from all walks of life. If everyone respects everyone else it will be an enriching, positive experience and we'll all have a great time. Fortunately, this group seems very receptive, a lot better than most. I help them put their food away in the kitchen and they head off for the beach. (As they leave I overhear one of the boys say to his councilor, "Jeff seems like a cool guy." That's a good sign!)

1:30pm. I do a sweep of the entire place and find that the new camp group has trashed the bathrooms in the back dorm. With twelve people using it all at once it can't be helped. I mop the floor again and re-do the men's dorm while I'm at it.

1:45pm. Time for my long-awaited afternoon siesta. Will I get it? I don't know because Raul is in the middle of a monologue about his restaurant job and he won't leave the Pequod. I'm hearing about which waiters are the best, and which ones still haven't been able to 'catch the system'. This leads into what the specials were last night, and that leads into all of the dishes Raul likes to make. His favorite topic is food and he can go on and on for hours about it. I've heard every word of this particular monologue before, and so exactly twelve hours after the last time I had to do this, I kick him out of the Pequod once again so that I can get some rest. I pass out immediately.

2:15pm. "Hey Jeff, are you in there?" shouts Osman from outside my window. I wake up with a jolt. He and Dallice are going for lunch and he wants to know if I want to join them. I tell him that I need to sleep.

3pm. My alarm clock wakes me up to the tune of another mild expletive. I'm not nearly rested enough, but I get up, get ready and open up the office early. The office doesn't officially open until 4pm, but from three to four I've already checked in the first eight guests. The phone is ringing off the hook the entire time, and I still need to wrap up the last load of laundry.

4:30pm. Our Italian guest has returned to pick up his belongings and check out, and the next three guests arrive.

4:45pm. The phone rings and it's my friend, Gary. Gary stayed with us at the beginning of the season while he was looking for work and housing. He found both, but now he's calling to tell me that his housing situation suddenly fell through and that he desperately needs a place to stay just for one night. He'll sleep anywhere he can. I tell him that he picked a hell of a day to do this, but that as long as we're at maximum chaos, why not? "Come on over and we'll see what we can do for you. I might have to offer you a tent." He says that's fine.

5:20pm. I've managed to return all of the phone calls that have piled up during the day and wrap up the last of the laundry. The phone has temporarily stopped ringing. I still haven't had the chance to check the e-mails, which on a normal day would be the first thing I do.

Tales from a Hostel at the Edge of the World

5:30pm. Ann arrives. Ann is a repeat customer. She was actually the first guest of the season and is exactly the sort of lovable, quirky individual that we generally attract like moths to the flame. She arrives with the usual dozen or so questions fired off in rapid succession, the answers to all of which she already knows. Right behind her is a hilarious group of five guys who have just arrived on their motorcycles. They say they've been coming here once a year for the past ten years to get away from their wives. I can tell they're going to be characters.

6pm. Our new camp group hasn't yet returned from the beach. This is good because Osman hasn't yet prepared the Endurance for them. He didn't start washing the sheets for them until after 4pm. By now the sheets are finished so I take them out of the dryer and head over to the Endurance. On my way out the door I hear one the boys from our other camp group tell his councilor that his bed has ants all over it. I put down the sheets immediately and have the boy show me his bed. Verily enough, his bed has ants all over it. This hasn't happened before. So we clear his bed, move him to another one, find a can of insecticide, and proceed to exterminate the entire community. The boys love it.

6:30pm. Osman and I finally attend to the Endurance and have it prepared for the camp mere moments before they return. I get the girls all settled in and then return to the office to find three hilariously dopey guys who have shown up without reservations looking for a place to stay. I have to explain to them that there is no way in hell that we can accommodate them tonight and I give them a phone book and the names of a few places in town. A few minutes later they return to me with a question: "Do you know how the phone book works?" I ask them if they're familiar with the alphabet. Then I look up the numbers for them. They're still figuring things out when our next guests arrive. I check them in and return to the desk to answer six more phone calls.

7:15pm. I still haven't had time to check the e-mail. In the meantime, some of the camp kids are trying to use the public computer, which is popping up error windows written in French before it finally crashes completely. This hasn't happened before. Not sure what the woman did to it this morning, but it doesn't seem to have stuck.

7:45pm. Gary shows up and I get him settled in the last available bed in the hostel, which has only become available because one of the camp groups showed up with one boy short. I tell Gary that this bed was previously covered with ants. He says that that's fine.

8pm. Things are finally somewhat under control. Osman and Dallice offer me dinner, which is a red fish curry that Dallice has just whipped up. It's marvelous.

8:15pm. The camp kids tell me that the computer is working again. Good.

8:30pm. The phone hasn't stopped ringing and the messages keep piling up. The camp kids keep buying sodas and Ann keeps asking me silly questions. In the meantime, people start coming up to ask about the news on the power outage. Apparently, somewhere out there in the real world, a major power outage occurred this afternoon that affected New York, Detroit, Toronto and Ottawa. I check the news to catch everybody up with the latest.

9:10pm. I finally check the e-mail: just five on-line reservations.

9:25pm. The kitchen has been trashed. Most of the dishes have been washed, but few have been put away. The sinks are clogged with food, and the counters are covered with crumbs. I start to get to work on the place and soon Gary shows up to lend a hand. Then some of the O'Shea's come in to help too. After a few minutes, the place is sparkling clean, and I make sure that everyone knows how much I appreciate their help.

9:50pm. I batch out the credit card machine and close out the register, answer one more phone call, take one more reservation and then close the office sharply at 10pm. I've decided that I'm going to sleep in the office, which has just enough space for a sleeping mat on the floor. It's actually quite a nice arrangement, affording me a little bit of privacy as well as two windows to let the air in. I put everything in place and find that it resembles a nice Japanese-style hotel room.

10:15pm. I join Osman and Dallice outside at the picnic tables for a clandestine beer. It's a perfect evening. The weather is cool and the ocean breeze feels delightful. The skies are clear again and the waning gibbous moon and the red planet Mars have returned to watch over us. After a while Osman and Dallice head off for the campsite in the woods, and then I hang out with Gary and one of the O'Shea clan for a little while before heading off to bed.

12am. The day is done. Every person has been accommodated and every challenge has been met. Even better, we've got a great group of guests in the house who all seem perfectly satisfied. The lights are out now, the hostel is calm and quiet, and I'm finally ready to fall fast asleep.

At the beginning of the season, when everything was fresh and usually under control, I was thoroughly convinced that we were running the best damn hostel in the U.S. of A., a claim that I was willing to announce publicly and with pride. But the past few weeks had been kind of rough. We had generally been overwhelmed and some days were definitely better than others. The challenges were ongoing, and both Osman and I had found ourselves rapidly approaching burn-out. About a week ago I had told Osman that I thought we might have lost the rights to our claim to fame and that we probably needed to tighten up our game. He reluctantly agreed. But today we got it back. Tonight, this was the best damn hostel in America once again. And I was very proud.

* * *

The season changes all around you. The signs are everywhere, but sometimes you just have to stop and take notice. The setting sun moves northward along the horizon as it approaches the solstice, pauses for a moment, and then slowly recedes again towards the south. The peepers in the marshes beyond the hostel slowly cease their peeping and soon begin travels of their own, leaving their wetlands to encroach upon the hostel. We find them on our houses in the morning dew. We find them in bathrooms, mop pails and, alas, occasionally in the washing machine.

Caterpillars turn into suicidal moths, dancing dangerously around the candles and lights at nightfall. Their numbers swell and reach a fevered pitch and then they too start to recede. June bugs come and go. Crickets emerge by the millions to play their surround-sound symphonies at dusk. The flowers have bloomed and then disappeared. Ivy appears stealthily and creeps around corners. The Big Dipper circles the North Star, the Milky Way wafts westward across the sky, the moon waxes and wanes. The one and only constant is the distant rumble of the North Atlantic as it crashes upon the shore, always sounding louder at night than it does during the day.

Chapter 9

Strange Birds

In which a flock of strange characters descends upon the hostel and bemusement and bewilderment ensue.

When Kayla and Jesse and their two-month-old son, Josh, showed up at the hostel, I immediately expected the worst. They were a very stereotypically dazed-and-confused young hippie couple from Colorado. Two rainbow children ragamuffins in dreadlocks, and not exactly among the sharpest kids I've ever met. They had made their reservations in advance, but when they showed up they had no money and no identification.

"We were wondering if we should bring our IDs with us," explained Kayla, "but then we just left without them…"

When they had made their reservations they had given us a credit card number and, upon arrival, Kayla very cavalierly told me to go ahead and charge their stay on it. But without the physical card in hand, I had no idea whose card it actually was. My first suspicion was that they were on the run from something. But the answer turned out to be that, in addition to having no credit card, no money and no ID, they also just had no sense.

I found out that the credit card number belonged to Kayla's mother, so I spoke to her over the phone. She assured me that everything was legitimate, that I could charge the card in her name and that she would fax me their picture ID's. So despite all appearances to the contrary, Kayla and Jesse weren't necessarily shady characters after all.

Or were they? They had met at a Rainbow Gathering, which was essentially a hippie commune pop-up phenomenon, and like so many other rainbow kids I had met before they were a bundle of contradictions, the sort of people who seem to be making a semi-conscious statement that they choose to live a lifestyle that is very self-righteously different from the crass material values of mainstream culture. But in my opinion, and certainly in the case of Kayla and Jesse, they often don't actually choose different values at all, but rather the worst values that modern society has to offer, namely a desire to profit as much as they can from other people at the least cost to themselves.

And that's what they proceeded to do from the moment they first arrived. In their starry-eyed manner they managed to mooch food, cab rides, and anything else their brains could conceive of from anybody who happened to be in their immediate vicinity. Indicative of their attitude, the morning after their first night at the hostel, Kayla noticed that there were a couple of cars parked outside.

"Whose cars are those?" she asked me. And without skipping a beat, "Can we get a ride into town?"

After I told her that she would have to get a cab if she wanted a ride into town, she decided she would share a cab with some of the other hostellers, a group of kids from Bulgaria. But from what I heard from them later, she apparently decided to share the cab, but not the fare.

As frustrating as it was to have these two in the hostel, and feeling as though it was somehow my responsibility to protect everyone from them, I soon realized that the situation simply was what it was, and that I really had no choice but to sit back and watch it all with some degree of amusement.

And amusing it was. Kayla and Jesse relentlessly made demands of everyone, and for whatever reason everyone seemed naturally to comply. One day our Dominican friends came back to the hostel to make us a rich, elaborate Dominican stew. Kayla and Jesse came in as we were enjoying our meal together.

"Is that soup good?" Jesse asked in his characteristic manner, his glazed eyes smiling and staring off into an unknown point in space.

"Sure," came the natural response from our friends who had never seen them before, "Do you want to try some?"

"I'll try some," said Kayla, "I'm starving!"

The soup was made with a combination of vegetables, pork, and chicken. Kayla went on to explain that sometimes she was a vegetarian and sometimes she wasn't, so today she would go ahead and have the soup.

Aside from their relentless demands, Kayla and Jesse were also amusing in other respects, Jesse in particular, whom I later nicknamed Pigpen. I always did my best to keep the hostel as neat and clean as possible, and I was truly astonished at how fast Pigpen could walk into a room and trash the place. Mere moments after they arrived, in fact, Jesse had ambled his way into the kitchen, found a large pot of oil that had been leftover from someone's cooking and immediately managed to spill its entire contents all over the kitchen and himself. Right away he asked if we would wash his clothes for him. Later highlights included images of Pigpen drinking coconut water out of coconuts, dribbling it all over his shirt, and later running though the yard in exhilaration during a flash torrential downpour.

Pigpen naturally had a way of tracking mud everywhere he went, and this was partially explained by his one, and apparently only, passion, which was to gather vegetation from the wild and turn it into food. In a way, I have to admit that I was rather impressed. One day he gathered cattails from the marshes and he beat them until he turned them into faux egg whites. Every day he would bring in bushels of plants and herbs and weeds he would find (leaving a trail behind him of course), and he would boil them and chop them up and cook them into some dish or another that he would then delightfully consume. One day he asked me which was the best beach on the island to find and gather seaweed. Regretfully I had to explain to him that I was no authority on the matter.

Undeniably, the saddest part about this little story was their two-month-old baby, Josh. Kayla and Jesse were clearly unfit to be good parents. Moreover, they bickered and fought with each other constantly and they would use the baby as a prop in their leveraging. Kayla would demand that Jesse stop being so negative because it would upset the baby. Jesse would take the baby and not hand it over to Kayla until he would get his way in a dispute, often causing the baby to cry. Kayla and Jesse clearly didn't actually get along and the baby was caught in the middle. The way I saw it, Josh's future could pretty much spiral in any direction. With parents like these, there was just no telling.

In the last hours of their stay, things got increasingly ugly. Jesse had wanted to spend their last day on the island in search of some sort of mystical plant. After a number of hours on this quest, Kayla had lost her patience for the venture and she wanted them to get back to the hostel with the baby before it got too cold and dark. Jesse was clearly unhappy about this and he made a point of making Kayla unhappy about it.

They argued about it all night, over a game of backgammon that took forever getting started because neither one of them knew how to set up the board. They would periodically go up to people in the hostel and ask each one to set up the board for them, but no one could oblige. They would see other people passing by outside and Kayla would send Jesse out to ask them to come in and set up the board. Robert and Jenna, our good neighbors from down the street, happened to drive by and they stopped their car to briefly say hello to Osman outside. When Kayla saw this she said to Jesse, "Go ask those people with car troubles if they know how to set up the board." Robert told Jesse that he wasn't sure, but that he thought it was black on one side and white on the other.

Somehow Kayla and Jesse eventually managed to get their game started and to complete their argument at the same time. In the end, Jesse decided that he was going to go out and find his plant in the morning, even if it meant abandoning Kayla and Jesse on the ferry off the island, on a trip that had been paid for entirely by her parents.

Kayla awoke in the morning and found Jesse gone. He had made good on his promise and she was furious. But she had to leave to catch her ferry at 10am and she asked me to call a cab for her at 9:15, which I did. While we were waiting she poured out all her grief to me, and I finally had the chance to console her a little bit, to back her up on the fact that she had every right to be furious, and that her obligation to her two-month-old child had to be her first priority, not her boyfriend from another planet.

While we were talking, Jesse phoned to tell her that he was on his way back to the hostel. And then her cab arrived. Her immediate response was to have the cab wait for an indefinite period of time until Jesse showed up. For the sake of the cab driver, I wouldn't have it. I put some other hostellers on the cab and told her I would call her another one. While she packed her belongings, which she somehow still hadn't managed to do at this point, she handed Josh to me. As I held the child in my arms, I fully felt the reality of his humanity, as well as an incredible sense of sadness for him and for his uncertain future.

Ten or fifteen minutes later, Kayla was continuing to pack, Jesse was continuing not to show up, and then the second cab arrived. Again Kayla wanted it to wait indefinitely, and again I told her that she couldn't do that.

And then from out of the blue there was Jesse, plant in hand! He had scrounged a ride off of a stranger and had made it to the hostel after all. The family was united once again. As they made their way to the car I gave Kayla an encouraging squeeze on the shoulder and wished her the best of luck. And then they were off and I breathed a huge sigh of relief.

* * *

Tales from a Hostel at the Edge of the World

From the very start of the season I had been receiving periodic phone calls from a woman named Maggie. Maggie told me that she had been coming to the hostel for several years and was always able to stay for free because she was an artist and would offer free classes to the other guests in exchange for her accommodation. I had a funny feeling about Maggie and felt that something was quite fishy about her story. In addition to the fact that such work exchange arrangements were 'officially' against the books, I also didn't think that it made any sense to give her a free ride just because she was going to hassle the other guests about art classes.

I called Martin and Larissa and they confirmed my suspicions. Maggie was just another crazy woman. Yes, she did return to the hostel year after year and, yes, she did try to stay for free year after year, but no such arrangements had ever been made. Time after time she kept calling me back, and I kept telling her that we weren't going to cut her any deals. Finally, she called to make a proper reservation and I put her in the books.

From the moment she arrived, I knew that we had another live one on our hands. It was the middle of the day when the office was officially closed. I was in the Pequod on a phone call with a friend in London when I saw a new guest arrive. When making reservations I always told people that we were closed during the day, and that check-in time was after 4pm, but when people arrived early I almost always just checked them in anyway. So I was planning on checking in our new guest just as soon as I got off the phone with my friend.

Instead what happened was that Maggie came straight up to my cottage and asked me to check her in right away. I found her a bit presumptuous, so I put down the phone and told her that we were officially closed until four. She claimed that she wasn't aware of this fact and reminded me that she and I had talked on the phone several times. At this point I knew exactly who I was dealing with and I also knew without a doubt that I had indeed told her when the check-in hours were. I brought this to her attention and she responded by telling me that last year the managers let her check in and hang out in the hostel even when it was closed. Sigh. Clearly what we had on our hands was not only one more erratic individual, but also someone with an inflated sense of entitlement.

I told my friend on the other end that I would call him right back and I took care of Maggie, explaining to her that I was happy to go ahead and get her settled in, but that in the future I would expect her to honor our closing hours. I then charged her for her and her son, Jake, a reclusive, adolescent misfit who had previously been sequestering himself in the shade reading a book. I settled Maggie in the women's dorm and offered to show Jake to the men's dorm, but he just stared at me blankly and said that he would wait until four. Fair enough.

Everything taken care of, I went back to the Pequod and rang my friend again. Minutes later, Maggie was back. I put down the phone and asked her what she wanted this time. She told me that she wanted to use our washing machine. As long as no one else was around she could go ahead and do her laundry, she informed me. After all, the previous managers let her do it all the time.

I told her that our single, small washing machine kept us constantly occupied with the linens and that we simply couldn't afford to make it publicly available or else we would never get our own work done. I offered to give her directions to the local laundromat, but instead what happened was that she pestered me until I couldn't take it anymore. It soon became easier just to let her do her laundry than to put up with her pestering. So I let her wash one load and told her that this would be the first and last time, and that I didn't want her taking advantage of my generosity or telling other guests that I let her use it.

By now it was quite clear that our new guest was not only quirky and needy, but that she was also very good at needling you until she got her way. And this was just the beginning. Maggie's special favors and requests continued relentlessly during the next couple of days and she distinguished herself as one of the most annoying personalities we had yet encountered. She also had a penchant for sneaking up on me with her requests. On more than one occasion, I would be doing work out in the yard, or sitting outside watching the sunset, only to suddenly realize that Maggie was hovering silently right behind me waiting to ask me for something.

And yet, in spite of all of this, there was still something somewhat charming about her that was impossible to explain. It was as if she was just so plain and up-front about her sweet and brazen requests that you almost couldn't hold anything against her. One day, as she was pestering me about acquiring another sort of special discount, I just glared at her in exasperation.

"Maggie…" I began.

"Hey," she cut in, "I'm a single mom. Every dollar counts."

Tales from a Hostel at the Edge of the World

If Maggie was an unusual character, her son was even more unusual. Jake was physically abnormal in an unfortunate way that simply couldn't be helped. But he was psychologically abnormal in a way that probably *could* have been helped. His book learning was out of this world. He was exceedingly interested in anthropology and linguistics and would deliver pretentious professorial monologues on these subjects to other guests, whether they liked it or not. When he found out that I had studied linguistics in graduate school that only encouraged him further.

On one occasion I tried engaging him in conversation, but his social skills were so non-existent that I soon found it impossible and ended up loaning him a book just to extricate myself. On another occasion, one evening a number of us were sitting around outside enjoying a bonfire. Jake soon showed up and started going on about the language families of Papua New Guinea until finally everyone had had enough. Instead of politely pretending to listen, people just started talking amongst themselves again. Undeterred, Jake simply continued his lecture to no one.

The impression that I got was that Jake was trying desperately hard to rebel against his unfortunate background. His mother was an airhead so he was determined to be an egghead. This theory was more or less born out by further observations. Jake and Maggie bickered constantly over anything and everything. She regarded him as an impossible child and he regarded her as an impossible mother. They were both right.

Maggie had told me that she wanted her new boyfriend to come join them on the island in the next day or two. She had met him the week before on another island in another hostel and three days later they had become engaged. She also told me that he had stayed at the previous hostel for three months in exchange for all of the hard work he did for them.

"That's just the way he is," she told me. "You'll see. So can he stay here for free also, right? He doesn't have a lot of money," she added.

I called the other hostel to verify her story and found it to be untrue. Maggie and her boyfriend had both stayed there, they continued, but they both paid for every night. Maggie is a pathological liar, they continued, and her boyfriend is crazier than she is, but completely harmless and actually a pretty nice guy.

Enter stage left, Bobby Faust, a.k.a. Neptune. When Neptune first called the hostel to leave a message for us, it went a little something like this: "Wassup, y'all? This is Neptune. I'm callin' you because Janet Jackson has invited me to your island. But I say, fuck it, I ain't goin' to that crazy island. I say, fuck it, I ain't comin'! But, you know what? Guess what? I *am* coming to your crazy island. You know why? Because I gots to see my baby, Maggie. She's a sweet, sweet lady, and I love her and I'm going to marry her. So fuck it, Neptune's comin' to town!"

This was just the first of several, highly bizarre, free-styling messages that we got from Dr. Neptune before he arrived. I had already been told that he was harmless, and we had certainly dealt with our fair share of lunatics and eccentrics before. Nevertheless, I was still a little apprehensive.

The next day I happened to pass by the desk as Osman was checking him in. Neptune had only just arrived but he was already telling tall tales to a captive audience. His name was Bobby, he said, but just after he had been born his mother held him in her arms and told those around him that he would be called Neptune. She then died from childbirth. He also told us that he had brought two birds with him to the island. They followed him everywhere he went and they were both ravens. He called one of them Raven and the other one he also called Raven. Nobody ever saw the ravens. He surmised that they were probably off exploring the island. He also told us that before he met Maggie he had been engaged to another woman. She had given him a diamond ring, but on his way to the island the diamond mysteriously split in half. That, he explained, was a sign from the gods that he was meant to be with Maggie and not with the other woman.

Oh yeah, for some unexplained reason, Neptune was also wearing a gold band around his head with a scratched-up CD attached to it.

I found Neptune's particular brand of crazy exceptionally amusing. Even more amusing were the reactions from other hostellers. The men liked him instantly. He was the sort of person who would take you aside upon first meeting you, tell you a dirty joke in the strictest confidence, slap you on the back and send you on your way. The women, on the other hand, were initially terrified of him. But after a little while, even they warmed up to his charms. The children found him fascinating and gathered around for his bizarre stories whenever they saw him. Neptune was surely one of the craziest guests we had ever had and possibly one of the most entertaining.

And so the little family had come together. From their interactions it was quite clear that Neptune loved Maggie, that Maggie was crazy about Neptune, and that Jake regarded them both with equal disdain. In the next two days these three unusual characters set off to explore the island, apparently making waves wherever they went. One evening I had decided to go into town to join Sarah and Jackie for a few drinks at a pub. We had struck up a conversation with a visiting tourist who independently brought up a story that she had made friends with these three crazy people named Neptune, Maggie and Jake. She went on to tell us that Neptune had shown her a picture of Jesus and told her that it was a picture of him. None of us were really that surprised.

The next day, after voluntarily scrubbing the hostel kitchen from top to bottom until everything sparkled, Neptune suddenly checked out of the hostel and left our lives as quickly as he had entered. It was way too soon. This was the craziest guy we had ever met and he left us all wanting more!

Out of a sense of morbid curiosity I was determined to get myself invited to the wedding and so I asked Maggie what their plans were. Alas, she told me, the wedding had been called off. She actually hadn't told Neptune yet because she thought he would be too devastated, but she had decided that it just wasn't that sensible to marry someone whom she had only met just a few days ago. After all, she said, not only did Neptune have a drinking problem, but he also didn't have any money. For a brief moment I was seized with the desire to try to change her mind, but I quickly thought the better of it.

Maggie and Jake checked out the next morning and I saw them off. Maggie gave me a big hug and Jake gave me a limp handshake. Parting is such sweet sorrow. Later that day I received the last lyrical phone message on the answering machine from Neptune: "Hey Jeff. This is Neptune! I wanna talk to Maggie, please. Let her know that I made it home. And everything's lovely. And right now we're just lookin' out at the stars in the sky. And I think to myself, what a wonderful world... Alright. I'll check wit' you later. Peace out."

Chapter 10

Bending the Rules

In which extraordinary people call for extraordinary measures.

From the beginning of the season to the end of the season, the nature of living and working at the hostel involved seeing many people constantly come and go. This could be a good thing when you had questionable guests. You always knew that they would leave eventually. But it could also be rather bittersweet. After all, the vast majority of our guests were lovely. So you would meet great people, feel like you're just getting to know them, and then they'd seem to be off just as quickly as they arrived.

So it was nice when guests I particularly liked would stick around for a while. There were, of course, rules on the books that officially limited anyone's stay to within a certain amount of time. But rules were made to be bended, and I would always make exceptions for exceptional people.

In fact, it was always interesting to see just how much importance any single human being could have on the environment. The hostel could be at full capacity, with fifty or so people running around, but any one bad guest always had the power to bring doom and gloom to a room, while any one good guest could always make the social environment so much more positive for everyone. Those were the ones that I liked. Furthermore, the longer a good guest would stay, the more stable that positive social environment would become.

Bill was exactly that kind of a guest. Dapper in style, charming and self-possessed, Bill came across as a true gentleman and a scholar, almost as if from another era. At the same time, when he first checked in he also seemed rather reserved. He would usually start his day by preparing a good healthy breakfast, he would clean up scrupulously and quietly after himself in the kitchen, most often cleaning up after other guests as well, and then he would get an early start on each day, exploring the town or hitting the beach. After a full day, he would return to the hostel to prepare a good meal for dinner, clean up and then go to bed early. It was quite clear from the start that he was a good guy with a good heart, but there didn't seem to be much of an opportunity to really get to know him.

After Bill checked in, one of the first things I noticed when checking the dorms each day was that he would make his bed each morning as though he were in the military. His bed was always the neatest and cleanest one in the room, whereas most of the other guys didn't even bother. However, with each passing day, it seemed that more and more guests in the dorm would start to follow Bill's lead. His was still the cleanest, but a culture of neatness and order was starting to develop around him.

But after more time had passed, Bill really started to open up. More and more, he was engaging the staff and the guests alike, and he turned out to be one of the most eloquent conversationalists I had ever met. He was intelligent and well-traveled, an avid reader and an art lover, with lots of curiosity about life and lots of experiences and wisdom to share. In fact, he was pretty much the picture of the perfect hosteller. Extremely versatile, he genuinely seemed to enjoy making the acquaintance of any of our guests, young or old, and of all possible backgrounds. And occasionally his fine art of conversation, plus his good looks and good humor, could even make the ladies around him blush!

Bill was just a great person to have around. His first visit to the hostel lasted ten good days. And as he worked for a school district in Connecticut, he had his summers off and he didn't live too far away, so he would return to the hostel frequently. All in good time, he would end up becoming both a familiar face and also a great friend.

Carolyn was another frequent flyer, quite literally. She worked for a major airline and, although she didn't much care for the day-to-day drudgery of her job, one of the perks was that she was able to fly for free to anyplace in the world. She often did, and she had great photos and stories as a result. And given that kind of freedom she was also able to catch a flight to the island at a moment's notice.

Carolyn's pet name for everyone was 'Pumpkin', and so we soon came to refer to her exclusively as Pumpkin. I adored Pumpkin's visits, we would have great times and great meals together, she was a fun and happy person to be with, and she was pretty much short-listed as a VIP from the moment she first arrived. Some people are just like that. If Pumpkin called and said that she was coming for the weekend, Pumpkin's name was in the reservation book. And if we happened to be sold out and didn't have any room for her, then by God, we'd make room for her!

Susan and Anne were like that as well. Susan was a true go-getter. Like Bill, she also worked for a school district, and so she could afford some good time off in the summer. But she was also an energetic mother of two, and it came as no surprise that she ran marathons as well. That was pretty much her spirit. I've rarely met people with such boundless and positive energy. And she was a great mom. She had left her son, Charlie, with her husband on this visit, but she arrived with her daughter, Anne, eight-years-old at the time, and a true delight. I liked them both instantly, pretty much from the moment they called to make reservations. When Susan first called, she asked if they could stay for a solid three weeks, which was unfortunately well over the acceptable limit.

And what a lovely time those three weeks were! I adopted them as my own right off the bat, and I had as much fun playing cards, doing jigsaw puzzles, and drawing pictures with Anne as I did bonding with her mother over trips to the beach and the occasional after-hours cocktail. And I was always happy to take care of Anne while Susan went for her morning runs. I felt that the three of us soon became an unconventional and fully functioning family. And I felt very fortunate that we would stay in touch for years to come, and that that summer would be their first of many visits to the island.

Now Gudrun was a funny one, at least initially. An older woman from Germany, she called towards the end of the season, not so much to ask for reservations, so much as to announce that she would be staying with us for a month. Her German accent was very thick and somewhat difficult to understand over the phone, and I didn't quite know what to make of her. But I did discern that she had been coming to the hostel for many years and that resistance was useless. We would have her at the hostel for a full month whether we liked it or not.

Gudrun arrived and immediately took over. Her first sense of outrage was over the state of the kitchen. When guests kept groceries in the fridges or on the shelves, we always asked that they labeled their food and that they either remove it or label it as free for all before they checked out. That was the theory but it didn't always work out that way in practice. And Gudrun was shocked, *shocked* by just how much food was unlabelled or had been left behind. (Mostly she just wanted the free food!) Having lived through wartime

Jeff Becan

Germany as a child, she could be incredibly resourceful with anything that was left behind.

So in true German fashion she applied a maniacal sense of order in the kitchen, which she strictly enforced. Although there were plenty of signs that spelled out the proper hostel etiquette for communal kitchen maintenance, Gudrun confronted each and every guest verbally to make sure that all rules were obeyed.

On the one hand, this wasn't typical behavior on the part of your average guest, but on the other hand the system had never worked so well! Gudrun was certainly pushy and felt that she had every right to take over, but she was also funny and lovable in her own quirky way. In any case, I didn't have any problems letting her wrest control and we ended up getting along famously. In fact, after a while, she started making dinner for me each night with whatever she could find in the kitchen. And it was usually quite good, which was fortunate for me since I never really had much choice in the matter.

So Gudrun and I ended up becoming great pals. Occasionally we would go to the beach together, and once or twice we attended church services together. On one occasion I actually let her take over the desk for me for a couple of hours so that I could attend to some other pressing matters. By that time she new the drill, and she was naturally thrilled to do it. After all, she had certainly made herself at home.

Towards the end of Gudrun's stay, my mother was planning on coming to the hostel for a visit. As I was preparing for her arrival, Osman asked me, tongue firmly in cheek, "So, what are you going to do when your *real* mom gets here?" As it happened, my two moms ended up getting along as well, and I was quite sad when they both had to leave.

* * *

At the beginning of the summer season, I had also learned that I had another trick up my sleeve that made good things possible for good people. As activity started to kick into full swing, the workload was becoming daunting. Although we were always flexible with our schedules, generally I would work most morning shifts at the desk, Raul would help with cleaning during the day, and Osman would work most evening shifts.

Tales from a Hostel at the Edge of the World

But notwithstanding phones ringing off the hook, full capacity crowds, and hostellers and groups constantly coming and going, there were always many other duties to attend to, accounting matters, physical maintenance issues, lots of yard work, etc. At a certain point, it all became a bit much for three people alone to handle.

And that's why God invented work exchange. Not always officially permitted, this can nevertheless be quite the fortuitous arrangement. The first time I allowed for this exception was right when the chaos of the season was just getting started. Raul was trying to clean the dorms while I was trying to mow the lawn, and although hostellers were asked to give us the space to do our work, the house was full and at any given moment people would often get in the way, a guest would have needs, or someone would arrive and want to check in early.

It was always something. And this time around it was a funky, orange Volkswagen camper van, complete with Grateful Dead and Phish stickers and a tattered pirate flag flying from the back. It pulled up to the hostel, past the designated driveway and straight over the yard to where I was mowing. I cut the power to the lawnmower as the van skidded to a stop, and out popped Tyler. Tyler was in his early twenties, a bit of a ragamuffin with crazy, long curly hair and a joyful gleam in his eyes.

Tyler told me that he had just arrived on the island for a job as a camp counselor. For the next two and a half months he would be working at a camp that led wilderness adventure tours for kids, hiking and rafting and fishing trips, where they would also learn about the nature and ecology of the island. The problem was that the camp didn't provide any accommodations for the counselors. Finding accommodation on the island wasn't cheap and at this point, somewhat later in the season, it wasn't easy either. Furthermore, Tyler didn't ask for much. He had everything he needed in his camper. All he wanted was a place to park it, and so he wanted to find out if he could possibly park it at the hostel.

Alas, even though I could tell that Tyler was a good kid with a good heart, I had to tell him that we couldn't really allow for that, primarily because camping like that wasn't strictly permitted anywhere on the island. Tyler was aware of this, but he had heard good things about the hostel and he figured that it couldn't hurt to ask. But oh well.

And then, as he was returning to his van to drive off in search of other possibilities, he stopped and turned around. "You know," he said, "I could always help out with the yard work in exchange. I love mowing and trimming and working outside…

We had an enormous yard to maintain, it took me about three hours to do the job thoroughly, and I usually had to attend to it once a week.

"Tyler, there's a discrete little space right behind the back building that would be perfect for your van. You'll need to clear out the growth and remove some of the debris and set it by the trash. Then I think we can come to some sort of arrangement."

Tyler took great care of all of the yard work for the next two and a half months. He was a great help and, to the extent that he was even around that much, he fit in perfectly at the hostel and was an especially big hit with our own camp kids. It was a fine arrangement, and it even gave him the opportunity to take a shower every now and then! When his job came to an end he was bound for Costa Rica for his next big adventure, but the whole situation had been quite beneficial. I certainly appreciated his help, which had come just when I needed it most.

Now work exchange wasn't anything I would ever take advantage of. But because it's such a common practice at hostels all over the world, we would constantly be getting e-mails and phone calls from random people asking if they could come and work at the hostel and stay for free. Sight unseen, I would never allow for this. But on a few rare occasions, if we had paying guests in the house who wanted to extend their stay for a day or two in exchange for some extra help, and if they would approach me discreetly (and if I happened to like them), there was usually never any harm.

Besides Tyler, the only other long-term exception was Heide. Heide was from Germany, she had just finished her degree in architecture, and she was just about to begin her first real job working for an architect's office back home. But between finishing school and starting work, she needed some time to herself. She had a great sense of mirth, but she could also be rather serious and intense. And it didn't hurt that she was adorable! I definitely took a shine to her and we soon developed quite a nice friendship.

Heide had booked her reservation for a week at the hostel, and as that week came to its end, she seemed to be getting more and more melancholy. Finally she told me that she was really sad to be leaving. She really felt like she needed more time on the island, and more time to be alone with her thoughts. Furthermore, her job didn't start for another three weeks, but as she had only just graduated college, she simply couldn't afford to extend her holiday any further.

Heide had absolutely no intentions of asking for any favors, so when I made her the offer her face lit up at once. True to form, she didn't accept it immediately. She wanted to think it through, make sure that she could change her flight plans, and make sure that it was the right thing to do. But eventually it all came together. To our collective delight, she stayed for another three weeks and she was not only a pleasure to have around, but she was also an incredible asset to the hostel. She primarily helped us with the cleaning, providing a woman's touch that had been sorely lacking, in addition to a proper German work ethic that far exceeded my own.

All of these great people came to enrich our lives at the hostel that year. Each of them brought something unique, but what they all had in common was a positive spirit and a love of the hostel. And as far as I was concerned, the longer they could stay the better.

Chapter 11

Season's End

In which it becomes time to close our doors, say our goodbyes, and sail off into the sunset.

The signs were everywhere. The days were getting shorter and the nights were getting colder. Different constellations were showing up in the night sky. We now had the beach to ourselves again. Fewer and fewer guests were arriving each day and the reservation book was starting to look more like it had at the beginning of the season, back before names were overflowing on every page.

The season had been filled with so many experiences: good, bad and bizarre, but overwhelmingly good. So many friendships had been born, so much bonding had occurred, and a lifestyle that for me had been truly extraordinary had also become quite comfortable. I had finally settled snugly into my new life, and now the season was rapidly coming to an end.

The return of the relative calm and quiet was good in many ways. For one, there was a lot of work that had to get done before the hostel could officially close its doors and settle into its winter hibernation. Rooms would have to get deep cleaned, all linens would get thoroughly washed and packed away with mothballs, and much of what had piled up over the course of the season would have to get cleaned up or discarded. I would also need to wrap up all of the accounting for the end of the season. Because we now had fewer and fewer guests we could get an early start on a lot of that work well before our last official day.

So there was a little more room to breathe. Time slowed down a bit and allowed us to get more accomplished at a more reasonable pace. For me it was also easier to get away from the hostel from time to time. I felt a little more comfortable actually leaving the hostel and going out for a night on the town with friends. That was all good.

And truth be told, it would also be good to get back to the mainland, back to 'reality', for lack of a better word. This had been an extraordinary and oftentimes challenging lifestyle, to be sure. But in other ways it was also something of a Neverland, for better or for worse. And as it happened, as wistful as I was becoming about the season's end, I was still undecided about whether or not I would return the next year. In many ways, island life and mainland reality seemed so far removed from each other that I felt that any decision I might make on the island might feel completely different once back on the mainland. Only time would tell, and that's exactly how I would leave it with my supervisors.

The hostel actually stayed open a little longer than many of the other businesses on the island, so by now we had already said goodbye to most of the friends that we had made over the course of the season. The Dominicans had left, the Irish had left, and the reunion alumni barbecues had come to an end.

And soon it became time to make plans. Osman and Dallice had both decided to stick out winter on the island. But they had also planned for a some off-island travels first and so they ended up being the first to leave. Osman had been a terrific First Mate and I knew that we would stay in touch. As for Sarah, she would stay on-island for a little bit longer before heading off on her own exotic travels before returning to Australia. Raul would also stay on a little longer at his restaurant before he returned to Florida for the winter. Meanwhile, Jackie and I decided to coordinate our travel plans and leave the island on the same day. We would then have some fun times together in Boston and New York before she headed back to Scotland and I headed off to Paris.

Time marched on and closing day at the hostel finally arrived. Soon the last of the work was finished, the doors were closed, and it was time to head off into the next unknown. I packed my bags and said goodbye to my favorite neighbors, Robert and Jenna, and then I took one last, long look around.

The place looked great. Good work had been done here this season, I thought, on every level. Difficult decisions had been made, but they had always been made in the best interests of the hostel and our guests. We had been a good team, we had served our guests to the best of our ability, and so much love and gratitude had been returned to us. Physically too, I thought that the place looked ten times better than it had when I first arrived. Lots of improvements had been made and I was quite pleased about that. But I was just pleased overall. Biased as ever, as far as I was concerned, this year this plucky little hostel had, in fact, become the best damn hostel in the U.S. of A. Case closed!

Helpful as ever, Raul gave me a ride down to the ferry terminal where Sarah and Jackie were waiting. Jackie and I then exchanged our hugs and our teary goodbyes with Sarah and Raul. And then it was time to board the ferry and say goodbye to the island.

It couldn't have been a sunnier and more beautiful day. Jackie and I got ourselves situated on the upper deck, the horn blew, and soon we were leaving port. We waved goodbye to our friends and then watched as the town receded.

En route to the open ocean, the ferry passes by a peninsula at the end of which sits a beautiful lighthouse. Jackie then told me about a local tradition of which I had been unaware. While rounding the lighthouse, she said, according to the lore, if you throw two pennies overboard into the water, you will be destined to return to the island. Fully prepared herself, she then handed me two pennies and pulled out two pennies of her own. I still had a little time to think about it, which I did. And then the moment came, we rounded the lighthouse, and we both threw our pennies overboard.

Chapter 12

The Fall and the Rise

In which I return to discover that the hostel has self-destructed and only a miracle can save us.

Six months later, after many travels and adventures, I was back at the hostel.

This season would see a brand new crew. During the winter, Osman had found a lucrative and more permanent position on the island. And as for Raul, although the two of us had eventually lost touch, I had just assumed that he was still in Florida. So it wouldn't be the same, but I also thought it would be good to start the new season with fresh faces.

Previously, as I had been pouring over resumes from new applicants, my brother, David, who was living in Chicago, had told me that he was looking for a change in pace. I told him I thought it would be a fantastic experience for us to live and work together for a season and, after a good deal of thought on his part, I was delighted when he decided he wanted to do it.

In regards to the other position, I had had someone else in mind who I thought would be perfect for the job. However, for unclear reasons, my supervisors chose to override my choice and hired a woman named Sally instead. I had seen Sally's resume, spoken to her on the phone and had also spoken to some of her references. She seemed nice enough, but there was really nothing extraordinary about her to make me think that she was the best choice. The decision to hire her was a rather frustrating situation for me that I honestly didn't understand, but I wasn't going to hold anything against her and I would certainly give her a fair shot. She would arrive at the hostel a few days after David and I were to get there.

During the off season we had arranged for some renovations to take place at the hostel. Because we had to leave the power and the water on for the work crew, we had also arranged for some on-island caretakers to shut everything down for the winter once the work was done. But as it happened, the water and heating systems had not been properly shut down and it had been a very harsh winter.

Jeff Becan

Immediately upon my return to the hostel I learned exactly what happens when you leave standing water freezing and expanding in copper pipes for months on end. As soon as I turned on the main water valve, and especially after I had the oil heating system back up and running, the entire infrastructure turned into a giant sprinkler system. We had leaks in almost every visible pipe running outside the buildings, and we had one major hot-water pipe running in the crawlspace beneath the floorboards of the main building that was functioning as a thermal geyser.

In other words, my hostel was in the process of self-destructing.

The obvious solution, of course, was to arrange for a professional plumber to come solve our problems. As it happens, the winter caretakers of the building had arranged for a plumber to come to the hostel the day that David and I were to arrive. However, on that appointed day, our journey had gone swimmingly until stormy weather had shut down all of the passenger ferries. Because of these delays, we wouldn't end up making it to the island until after nightfall.

Once I realized that this was the case I made sure that the message was passed on to the plumber. I checked back later and was told that the plumber would meet me the following morning instead. For mysterious reasons, he never did and he never would.

With just a few days to go, it now seemed very unclear whether we would be able to open up in time for our first guests. The only good news was that I soon found a volunteer who knew a little bit about plumbing and he was able to help repair some pipes, replace other pipes, and teach me a few things in the process. The bad news was that there were so many more pipes to fix and there seemed to be no good way to even access the major pipe underneath the main building. The only short-term solution was to cut off the water to that pipe, which also cut off water to most of the hostel.

After many desperate attempts, I finally found another plumber who said that he'd be around first thing the next morning to take a look at what we needed to get done. What a relief, I thought. The guy seemed nice enough over the phone and I felt confident that things were about to fall into place.

But somehow the next morning the guy showed up playing the part of Tony Soprano. He and another guy took a good look around the place and then they proceeded to verbally accost me about how bad the job was and how they didn't have any time to do it. Tony then went on to tell me that, no offence, but he was pretty pissed off at 'this place'. He claimed that he had done all of the plumbing work on the hostel years ago, he knew exactly where everything was and what needed to get done, but we never called him last year to do any work, so why should he do anything for us now? (The answer was that we didn't need any plumbing work done last year.) His angry monologue continued to replay itself as he and his buddy headed back to their van. Once more he told me, no offence, but he was still pretty pissed off. Then they drove off.

A bit dazed and confused at this point, I nevertheless proceeded to call around to more plumbers on the island, but not a single phone call was returned.

The following day an older couple from the neighborhood dropped by to say hello. We chatted for a while and, as they were leaving, I asked them if they happened to know any good plumbers. This seemingly innocuous question seemed to catch them both off guard. They glanced nervously at each other and told me that they were sorry, they didn't, and that it was *very, very* difficult to get a plumber on this island. They then wished me good luck and hastily made their exit.

I continued to leave messages for plumbers and waited for them to call me back. Nobody did. Later, however, another neighbor dropped in to say hello and I told him what I was dealing with. He told me not to worry. He was staying in the house next door with a buddy of his, who just so happened to be a plumber. He told me he would come back with his friend to see if they could help me out. Hours passed, but eventually they both came by.

The plumber friend took a look at what we were dealing with, gave us some advice about what needed to be done, but then said that he couldn't do it because his back hurt. However, he did write down for me the name and number of another plumber that he recommended. Having seen by now just how *very* difficult it was to get a plumber on the island, it occurred to me that I might have better luck if I could call this new contact and drop his friend's name as a reference. However, we hadn't been properly introduced so I casually asked plumber friend what his name was. He replied, "I'd rather not say." He then attempted to give me a cryptic explanation about it being a long story, but that he just wasn't comfortable giving me his name. Then they both left.

Word of my difficulties got around to my supervisors and they gave me a few more leads. I called Martin and he told me to call John Brown, a plumber who had worked out for him in the past. "John might do it," he said. "But just be sure you don't call his brother, Manny. Those two guys hate each other, plus ain't no way in hell Manny would come 'round." I called them both. Same story. No messages returned.

The next morning the phone rang and it was someone who wanted to make reservations at the hostel for himself, his son, and a friend of his. In a funny and delightfully high-pitched voice, he told me that they actually wanted to come over the next day. I explained to him that this would be impossible because we weren't actually scheduled to open for three more days. Moreover, even that was looking increasingly dubious given the fact that we were suffering the slings and arrows of outrageous plumbing fortune.

Then he told me that I was in luck. He was a plumber by trade, he loved our hostel, and he was more than willing to come and help us out. I explained our problems in further detail and he said it would be a piece of cake. I told him to come as soon as he could and that if he could help us solve our problems then he could stay for free for as long as he liked. He told me he'd get back to me by the end of the day.

He didn't.

By this point, my brother had convinced me of a massive conspiracy taking place. Perhaps it was bigger than we could possibly comprehend. Perhaps unwritten rules had somehow been violated. Perhaps there had never been any plumber on the phone at all. It could have been a mad delusion on my part. Or maybe the man on the phone was just another mysterious actor in this vast conspiracy. Perhaps, unbeknownst to us, it was National Plumbers' Practical Joke Month. All I knew was that I could no longer be sure of anything.

The next morning the phone rang again and it was the same guy. He told me that they were on their way to the island and that he was hoping to catch the 11am ferry. That would put him on the island by around 1pm. So I hadn't dreamt it up after all!

Or had I? The hours passed and no one came. The sun began its slow westward descent. I decided to call this guy's cell phone number but got no answer. All was lost. Up was down and down was up. *There was no plumber!*

And then, just when I had given up all hope, that night our plumber, Brad, arrived with his friend, Frank, and his adorable six-year-old son, Noah. Their arrival was a godsend. Brad and Frank were loud, colorful, jovial characters who generated contagious laughter from the moment they arrived.

Tales from a Hostel at the Edge of the World

They entertained us that night with loads of hostel and travel stories, and Noah kept us amused with the sort of antics you can only get from a six-year-old boy.

The next morning we all got to work. Brad soon saw that all of the problems were much more serious than he had previously thought, but he wasn't daunted. Frank and I assisted him diligently and I ended up learning all kinds of mad new skills before the day was over. A long, grueling day it was, but we eventually got all of the holes repaired, all the faulty pipes replaced, the thermal geyser was a thing of the past, and hot water was available all over the hostel. By the end of the day we were absolutely exhausted, but we had done some damn good work. And thanks entirely to Brad, my new best friend and guardian angel of plumbing, we were now ready to open with honor and dignity, and just in the nick of time!

Chapter 13

Turbulence

In which a young girl falls down a hole and a series of unfortunate events ensues.

Sally had arrived in the midst of all the plumbing fiascos. As I didn't actually hire her in the first place I didn't have much of a read on her either. As far as I was concerned, she was a wild card. I suppose my only first impression was that she seemed quite young and girlish. My only other first impression was a curiosity about the fact that she wore tennis shoes with long laces that she always left untied.

The first day on the job, Sally tripped into a hole.

In order to access the most furious pipe, we had had to get into a crawl space underneath the main building. There was a large trap door on the floor in the kitchen that provided access, and it was pretty obvious to everyone else that the trap door was open and blocked off. Nevertheless, Sally managed to fall through it anyway and she got a small but fairly deep cut on her shin in the process. The next day, at her request, I took her to the hospital, where they couldn't really do much for her but come up with ways to make her minor injury cost our outfit almost a thousand dollars.

It was a simple mistake, and everybody makes mistakes. But unfortunately it wouldn't be the last. In fact, it soon became clear that the one thing Sally excelled at was making mistakes. There were mistakes with common register transactions that I would correct repeatedly. Sally also had difficulties committing things to memory. That was OK because I had put together an instruction manual the previous season in which I had spelled out every possible process, which she always consulted. For example, when we closed the register at the end of each day, we would put in a certain key, then press two keys in succession, and this would generate the nightly report. After about a week and a half, Shelly had yet to memorize this step. She could get as far as the first step and then she'd have to consult the book.

Competence is always a good quality to look for in any employee, but perhaps even more important were the social skills required for this line of work. One day a young Japanese woman arrived at the desk to check in. Sally greeted her by saying, "Hi! My name's Sally. What's yours?" Our guest responded with a difficult, multi-syllabic Japanese name, to which Sally reacted with a pause, a giggle, and then, "OK?" After checking this woman's passport, Sally then handed it back to her and said with a grin, "You look like a doctor!" Everyone was confused.

On another occasion, a wide-eyed Bulgarian kid showed up at the hostel to ask if he could see a friend of his, a young Bulgarian woman named Eva, who was staying with us at the time. It seemed obvious to me that this was a guy who presented no problems whatsoever, who simply wanted to see his friend, but Sally regarded him with visible suspicion and mistrust.

"What is this in regards to?" she grilled him, "May I ask just *why* you want to see her?"

I didn't find this to be the sharpest judgment call and neither did anyone else. I called Eva down and she was happy to see her friend, whom she had been expecting in the first place.

Furthermore, earlier that season I only had to evict one person, a very strange guy, probably a derelict, whose erratic behavior was simply making all of the other guests nervous. I probably shouldn't have admitted him in the first place, but the reason he had come to the hostel initially was because Sally had met him in town and had invited him to stay at the hostel.

In spite of my frustrations, I did my best to deal with Sally patiently, and I initially thought that we could work on all of these problems with enough attention and time. But it was not to be. What it came down to in the end was that Sally was basically a sweet, innocent kid who was just in the wrong place at the wrong time. She was a little odd and a little immature, but there was nothing dislikable about her. In fact, I did like her! But if she couldn't get a grip on either the routine or the social skills needed at this point in the season, when the job more or less felt like a vacation, then she simply wasn't going to be able to cut it once we really got going.

So once again, at the start of another season, it soon became evident that I really had no choice but to let another employee go. I explained the situation in depth to my superiors and they backed me up on it. This was good since they were the ones who had created this whole unfortunate situation in the first place.

In any case, I wanted to be the one to handle it because I wanted to approach the endeavor with as much humanity as possible. I not only sympathized with Sally; I *grieved* for her. It wasn't fair to her that she was placed in this situation. So I dropped hints and expressed concerns and tried to give her every possible cue that things weren't going so well. I could also tell that she was getting frustrated with her own performance.

Eventually I decided to initiate the process by contriving a written self-evaluation. I drew up a set of questions that I gave to her and I asked her to take her time, fill out the form and then get back to me in a day or two and we would talk about everything. Two days passed and I approached her about it, only to discover that she had spaced out and forgotten about the whole thing.

"Never mind," I said, "let's just have a talk…"

I had prepared myself for the ordeal to go in one of two ways. Either Sally would have picked up on the cues like I wanted her to, with the distant possibility that she might offer her resignation first and spare me the grief of letting her go. Or she wouldn't know what was about to hit her. It turned out to be the latter.

I did my best to be as compassionate and honest and gentle as I could be, but in spite of my best efforts, the end result was that Sally was caught in a train wreck and I was the train. The fates had decided that I was to play the role of Kali, the Hindu goddess of death and destruction, burning the universe and savaging the innocent in order for the world to be reborn anew.

It sucked.

Sally packed her bags and left the next morning. We had a few more heart to heart conversations before she left. Neither one of us could determine who felt worse about it all. The cab soon pulled up, I helped her with her bags, and we even shared a good hug before she was off. I didn't feel any better about it. I later found a note that she had left for me that started, "Life goes on. I will go on. I will move on into the real world instead of the dream world I've been drifting in…"

Instead, she unexpectedly moved in with a questionable character whom she had met at the hostel and who was old enough to be her father. David and I both knew the guy and regarded him as a possible psychological predator, if not the devil himself, but apparently Sally was head over heels about him. She sent me e-mails afterwards and told me that everything was fine. She also made a point of telling me that her parents knew all about it. I didn't believe a word of this and it turned out not to be true.

I remained genuinely concerned about her. At the time, my friends and advisors told me to remember that, at twenty-three years old, she was technically an adult and was responsible for her own decisions. I didn't buy a word of that either.

Fortunately, I did continue to have occasional correspondence with her, and I eventually learned that she had moved out of the creepy guy's house, she had moved on in her life, and she was pursuing a career path that seemed to suit her perfectly. I sincerely hoped that everything that happened had happened for the best.

In the aftermath of all of this, the immediate good news was that I found a much more suitable replacement for her in the form of a long-term guest of ours who couldn't have been more perfect for the job. Her name was Amy, she started the day after Sally left, and she was fantastic. She and David and I not only made a crack team professionally, but personally we couldn't have gotten along better. It had certainly been a turbulent beginning of the season, but now the world had been destroyed and the world had been renewed and life would indeed go on.

Chapter 14

Something About Mary

In which a curious guest develops a curious condition and then promptly vanishes into thin air.

Our hostel certainly received more than its fair share of oddballs from time to time, from the harmless eccentrics to the occasional schizophrenic to the bad eggs who sometimes had to be removed by force. Mary was sort of a cross between the eccentric and the schizophrenic. As it happened, I had met Mary the previous year, in the course of my own travels, while staying at another hostel on the mainland.

Mary was a petite middle-aged woman with boundless energy reserves. Immediately upon introducing herself to me, she had launched into a rambling and absurd and wholly entertaining stream of consciousness speech about God only knows what. She was one of those people for whom it seems there is no barrier between the thoughts inside the head and the words coming from the mouth. I simply did my best to roll with the punches and engage her accordingly. Mary was definitely an oddball, but like so many others, she was a likable one in her own way.

Almost a year later, from out of the blue, Mary showed up at our own hostel, her same old crazy self. She arrived without reservations and, true to form, she didn't spare any time before introducing herself to everyone in the house and delivering her rapid-fire, crazy monologues. Most relatively normal people were initially freaked out, then gradually acculturated, and then utterly resigned before coming to the conclusion that there was actually something really nice about this crazy lady, a really positive vibe underneath all the bizarre mental goings on.

The morning after she arrived, Mary headed out to wander the island aimlessly, and when she returned to the hostel that evening she looked a fright! Of Irish descent, she had light red hair and fair skin, and she claimed that being in the sun all day had caused her face to swell from sunburn. It was swollen beyond belief and it was really, really unsettling. Quite concerned, I did some searching and soon discovered that she had developed a condition called facial edema, also rudely known as *moon face*, which is a fairly accurate description. You could barely see her eyes underneath her bloated skin.

But Mary immediately waved the whole thing off, saying that she had just gotten a sunburn from being outside and that it didn't hurt at all. And then she went on to describe her day of wandering the beach, taking random turns, somehow getting lost and finding herself on a golf course, eventually finding her way back to a road, miraculously ending up at the grocery store where she wanted to go anyway, and then wending her way back to the hostel. I'll spare the rest of the details. There were many.

My research on moon face yielded the information that it could be caused by many factors, including overexposure to the sun, and that as long as there was no pain or difficulty in breathing, it would generally pass with time. Still, by the next afternoon Mary's condition had only gotten worse. Amy tried to talk to her to suggest that she take it more seriously, but she didn't get far before Mary told her that it was really nothing to worry about and then she changed the subject to her adventures at a bar that day, the people she had met, and a play-by-play of every interaction accompanied by running commentary and analysis.

Later that night I took my turn. I told Mary that I remained concerned about the swelling and she immediately started making the same maneuvers, launching into other topics of conversation. I just decided to interrupt her until I forced her to tell me whether or not she was on medication (she claimed she wasn't), whether or not this had happened to her before (she claimed it hadn't), whether or not she was experiencing any pain or shortness of breath (she claimed she wasn't), and finally wedging in my conviction that if it persisted or became worse I would pressure her into going to get checked out at the hospital. She was surprisingly receptive to this, which was good, so I rewarded her with a few moments of rapt attention to some more of her rambling stories.

Fortunately enough, by the next morning the swelling *had* gone down a little bit. She still looked a fright, but at least it seemed to be getting better instead of worse. By around midday Mary headed forth for another day of exploration and adventure.

It turned out to be another busy day at the hostel with lots of activity, lots of work to get done, and before I knew it we were closing up the office for the evening. It wasn't until I was on my way to the Pequod that it suddenly occurred to me that Mary hadn't returned to the hostel. David and Amy realized this at the same time, and after a little while one of our other guests came knocking on my door to raise the same concern.

With anyone else this would not have been a cause for concern, but with Mary it was a different story. I called the police non-emergency line, explained the situation, and asked if they might have any information. They didn't, but they suggested that I call the emergency room at the hospital. The hospital had nothing on her either. One of her stories from the previous day had been about how much fun she had had at the bar, so I decided to call the bar she had been talking about. They recognized the description and told me that she had made quite an impression, but that she hadn't returned since. By midnight, not knowing what else to do, I called around to every other place in town that might still be open, but nobody had any information on her.

A truck soon pulled up in our driveway and we all ran outside to see if it might be her. It wasn't. It turned out to be another one of our guests, Esteban, who was a really good guy. Naturally, he asked what was going on, and after I told him he offered to drive me around town to look for her. Esteban and I checked out all the usual spots but found no signs of her. In fact, the entire island seemed eerily deserted.

After we got back to the hostel, David and Amy took a flashlight and went down to the beach to see what they could find: absolutely nothing. The fog had rolled in by now and there was very limited visibility. By the time they returned it was nearly 2am. And the situation was simply this: Mary had disappeared without a trace, leaving her bed made with her nightgown laid out on it, we might never see her again, and there was nothing more we could possibly do. I decided that if she didn't come back by the next morning, after the official period of twenty-four hours, I would go ahead and file a missing person's claim.

The next morning I did just that. An officer arrived promptly and we told him everything we knew. He said the police would start by combing the beaches and then they would get back to us. They ended up finding nothing, but there would be a couple more follow up visits during the day.

Later on, Amy suggested that Mary might have just gotten on a ferry and left the island. After all, she had originally planned on leaving this morning anyway. So I called the ferry terminal, gave them the whole song and dance, and asked if they could tell me anything. The person on the other end said that she wasn't legally permitted to give me any information, but that she could talk to the police. I called the officer on the case and left him a message relaying this information.

An hour or two later, the cop car pulled up to the hostel again and our officer told us that they had followed the lead and discovered that Mary had, in fact, left on the morning ferry. He told us that there was no record of her name but that she matched the description. Apparently, he said with a smirk, she had made quite an impression! There was a collective sigh of relief. If we knew nothing else at all, at least we knew that Mary was alive, somewhere in the world.

Because Mary had arrived without reservations, I had never had a phone number, nor was I able to obtain one by calling information. But two or three days after this all happened, Mary called the hostel! Amy answered the phone and was delighted to hear from her. Mary talked to her for probably half an hour, telling her that she had just decided to leave the island early, that sometimes she just acts on whims like that, and that she was sorry if she might have been a little crazy from the heat while she had stayed with us. She then went on to detail some of her more random adventures and closed by saying that the reason why she had called in the first place was because she had seen a movie on television that took place on a tiny island. But isn't that crazy, she went on, because she had just come from an island, a tiny island, really, when you think about it…

So all was well that ended well. Mary was alive, we were happy, and we all hoped that we might even get to see her crazy self at the hostel again someday.

Chapter 15

The Best of Times

In which a collection of colorful characters underscores, once again, just how wonderful the world of hostelling can be.

David and Amy and I ended up making a marvelous team. All three of us loved our jobs and loved the hostel and wanted it to be the best that it could possibly be, which it was. This season was even busier than the previous season, but as demanding as the job could be, there were still many times when it felt to all of us that the hostel was practically running itself. We rose to all of the challenges, we were good at what we did, and we had a great time doing it.

And we had some terrific guests. The early part of the season saw the arrival of a whole new slough of international seasonal workers, many of whom became great friends. Alejandra was one of the first. She was a delightful woman from Costa Rica, with a perpetual twinkle in her eye, who came to the island to find work in gardening and landscaping. She found jobs right away and generally worked from sunrise to sundown. As a result it was hard for her to find the time to look for housing and she ended up staying with us for over a month. But during that time she became a part of the family. As much as I wanted her to find permanent housing we were all sad once she finally did. Fortunately she was able to come back and visit from time to time.

Naturally we saw many Irish and Bulgarian kids return, but this year we also met a cast of Hungarians, all of whom were great fun. Sylvester was their ringleader, which was not surprising. He was tall and thin, with short dark hair and dark eyes and a goatee that made him look mildly diabolical. On top of that he had a deep voice reminiscent of Bela Lugosi. But he also had a terrific spirit and a wicked sense of humor and he quickly became one of our best friends. Sylvester had heard great things about the island and he decided not only to make the journey himself but he also convinced about five of his friends to join him on the adventure. They were all fantastic.

Jeff Becan

One of my favorite peculiarities of Sylvester's was his use of the verb 'to make'. He was constantly 'making' things that one doesn't typically 'make' in English. Coming to the island in the first place was something of a daunting challenge but, he said, in his ever so deep and amusing accent, he had decided to 'make a chance' anyway. One night he and his friends cooked us up a traditional Hungarian goulash. After he sampled it he decided that it wasn't very good at all, but he reluctantly shared it with us just the same and suggested that we simply 'make a chance'. It was sad when the Hungarians eventually got sorted and left the hostel, but Sylvester promised me that they would return often to 'make a party' and he made well on his promise.

We continued the tradition of weekend barbecues for our beloved alumni and one night was just exceptional. We had had a great meal outside and several old friends had been able to join us. As the sun set and it got colder we moved everybody into the Pequod, where we continued to 'make a party' that soon turned into a treasure trove of a talent show. David began by regaling the crowd on guitar and vocals, singing some early American folk songs he had been learning. Then Sylvester took the guitar and he and his friend, Marti, broke into some amazing Hungarian folk songs. The Irish weren't to be left out and four of our Irish girls, Maeve, Marcella, Jane and Grainne, then overwhelmed us with some beautiful traditional Gaelic numbers, all sung a cappella. Marti followed this with some Broadway tunes, David brought out an Argentinean ballad on his guitar, and it just went on and on into the night. It was an incredibly beautiful evening that once again underscored just how wonderful the world of hostelling can be.

We saw some crazy characters as well. Peter and Blue arrived with a bang. One afternoon the front doors barged open and in they flew. "Hey everybody, the party has arrived!" announced Peter as they bypassed the reception desk, threw their bags on the floor, and literally jumped sideways into the chairs in the common room, sunglasses still on and bottles of rum in hand! They had just gotten off their flight from Bermuda, which they had apparently turned into a rollicking party that they had every intention of continuing at the hostel. They were absolutely hilarious and I reluctantly had to explain that our policies required a little more discretion. Especially at three in the afternoon.

Eventually they sobered up enough to check in and we got them sorted. Peter was a tan, silver-haired Englishman, quick witted and sharp as a tack. Blue was a beady-eyed man-child from California. Together they made a most unusual and amusing duo, straight out of the pages of Steinbeck. They both lived in Bermuda, where they were avid practitioners of kiteboarding. They had come to the island for a week to take a certification course to become kiteboarding instructors, but the bad news was that the endeavor depended rather a lot upon the wind.

And there wasn't a whole lot of wind that week, which was unusual. Each afternoon after they rolled out of bed Peter would come into the office to check the latest weather forecast, while Blue would just stare longingly into the sky, asking, "Dude, where's the wind?" There was only so much they could do without it. Each day they hoped expectantly, each night they went barhopping, and day after day the wind was nowhere to be found. Spirits and sails were becoming more and more deflated.

And then, with just two days to go, the wind rolled in again! Peter and Blue were ecstatic. They were finally able to do what they needed to do in order to complete the course, they passed with flying colors, went out on one last bender to celebrate, got lucky with a couple of ladies, and soon they were back on the plane to Bermuda, no doubt continuing the party all along the way. Part of me was quite relieved to see them go; another part of me wished I were going along with them!

I was fortunate that we had hardly any bad eggs this season, especially compared with the season before. We did have one extremely nasty character in the form of an old curmudgeon called Glen, who showed up at the hostel and proceeded to complain about every aspect of how we were running it from the moment he arrived until the moment he left. His unconditional criticisms were so unrelenting that, for the first time in my life, I found myself wanting to take a shovel to another person's head. (It wasn't a great feeling.) What was gratifying, however, was that as he spewed out his vitriol to each and every guest we had in the house, all of them countered him and told him that they thought that this was a great hostel and that we were all doing a terrific job. It's nice when you can please most of the people most of the time!

I was also grateful to have a lot of old friends returning. Pumpkin continued to fly in on weekends as often as she could. Bill came back for two more excellent long visits. This year Susan returned with Anne as well as Anne's little brother, Charlie. Having Anne and Charlie around was just loads of fun and we logged hours upon hours of card games, jigsaw puzzles and bellyaching laughter. Brad, my plumbing hero, also came back for more visits, bringing his jovial family and friends back with him. And, of course, towards the end of the season, Gudrun would also return to take over general operations for another month.

Another old friend who returned was a lovely woman from Boston named Frances. Frances had only visited once before during the previous season, and I liked her right away, so I was glad that this year she returned on three separate occasions. She was a gentle soul with a delightful sense of humor and a keen eye for the subtle beauty of the natural world. While I took inspiration from the grandiosity of the sea and the sky and the gusting winds, Frances helped me to appreciate the smaller wonders that our natural environment had to offer. We would spend many an evening pouring through the hostel's library of nature guides to identify different types of seashells and various egg casings and seaweed and all sorts of beautiful little gifts from the sea that Frances would discover during the day. Her visits were always a pleasure.

On her last visit of the season, Frances left a note that I treasure to this day. It went something like this…

Dear Jeff,

This island is very beautiful so I returned here this year in June. And I came back in August and October because of the feeling of the hostel, which is due, in large measure, to the spirit that all of you give to it.

One night in June (and there were not many people staying at the hostel) you and I and a few others were reading in the living room and I felt very much that this place felt like a home. Maybe that is natural because it has been your home for several months now.

For reasons that are too complicated (or perhaps too subtle) to explain, I was also very moved by your plumber friend, Brad, and the family prayer that he led just this morning, how he is teaching his sons how to live right. Now that is a good man doing right in the world. And you are a good man doing right in the world too by your generous and happy spirit.

I have had a wonderful time here and I suspect we will see each other next year on this beautiful island. Have a good autumn, take good care, and many thanks.

Tales from a Hostel at the Edge of the World

Sincerely, Frances

Along with the note she left some more small treasures and added this postscript:

P.S. I gave you knobbed whelks earlier this year; these are channeled whelks - different egg cases!

With dear friends like Frances and so many others, and with great comrades-in-arms like David and Amy, it had been a fantastic season and the state of the hostel had never felt more positive, warm and gratifying. For the second year in a row, once again, we were the best damn hostel in these United States! Of this I was sure and it was a great feeling.

And then it was suddenly somehow fall again! Somehow this season seemed to have flown by as if in fast forward. The hostel eventually closed its doors once more. We left the island together and boarded the ferry back to reality on a cold, rainy day.

But unlike the previous season, this time I was leaving with a good amount of certainty. This time I was determined to return for one more season, but I was also determined that it would be my last. One more time around next year was in order, and then it would be time to move on to life's next chapter, whatever that might be.

Chapter 16

Return of the Plumber

In which yet another disaster befalls the hostel and hitherto unknown powers are discovered and unleashed.

And so, all in good time, it was back to the hostel for a third and final season.

This time, unlike the others, my plan was to arrive with ample time to spare in order to take care of business, as well as any unforeseen emergencies, well before the season began. And this time, unlike the others, I would also arrive just by myself and with no one waiting for me. I was looking forward to this. Social creature that I am, I relish my solitude every bit as much as I relish the company of others, and so I was very much anticipating getting back to the island, getting back to the hostel, putting things in order, and then basking in the peace and serenity and the glow of the island as it is in its quiet, pre-season state. The idea was to arrive before sunset, turn the water and the heat on and then settle down for a quiet evening before a busy day of preparations in the morning.

We all know, however, that things don't always turn out the way you planned them.

At the end of the previous season, we had arranged for still more renovation work to be done after we closed, but this time we were told that the crew wasn't going to need the water, heat, or electricity. That meant that we could shut everything down properly and so I had called Brad out to help. He and I had taken every necessary precaution and I was thoroughly convinced that we would have nothing left to worry about in the spring.

Instead, when I returned to the hostel, I not only found all of the buildings unlocked, but I also discovered that someone, at some point in time, had turned the main water valve on after we had shut it off. This should not have been done and whodunit was anyone's guess. I honestly didn't care. What I cared about was how I was going to fix what seemed to be at least three really, really bad leaks in three very, very crucial locations.

Jeff Becan

I went through the usual stages: grief, denial, acceptance, more grief. I already knew from the previous year that I wasn't going to get a plumber, and so I wasn't even going to try. I did anyway. Just for form's sake. Left a message that didn't get returned. Just to make sure that the system was still in place, really. I also knew that even if I could get Brad out it would still take him a number of days just to get everything in order, and I didn't want it to take a number of days. This was too big of a problem to let it wait.

My good neighbors, Robert and Jenna, and their new beautiful six-month-old daughter, Nena, commiserated with me that night and ended up showing me every possible courtesy in the days ahead. After discussing with Robert all of my non-options for solving the problem, he finally responded with, "Well, I guess you don't really have any choice but to do it yourself."

This totally took me off guard. My instinctive reaction was that I couldn't imagine pulling it off. Sure, I had replaced my fair share of pipes the previous year, but it was practically always under Brad's tutelage. I wasn't even going to entertain trying to take a chance on this all by myself, with the stakes this high, and with no one there to check my work. It was one thing just to remember the basic steps, but plumbing is an art as well as a science, and I just didn't think…

That night I dreamt that I fixed all the pipes, and so I woke up resolved to fix all the pipes. Or at least try. The first of the three pipes was in the back building, above ground and very accessible. If I was going to take a crack at this then I would start with the easiest one. If I could pull that one off, then maybe I would try the others. So I gathered up my tools and took the plunge. I don't know how long the first one took. I lost track of time. But as I was wrapping it up the foreman from the renovation crew dropped by to say hello. He asked me what I was doing, I explained, and he wished me luck.

"Remember," he said, "All you have to do is turn the water back on when you're finished and if it doesn't leak then you did it right."

I think that this was meant as encouragement, and I accepted it as such, even though it wasn't true. Use too little solder and you still have a leak, use too much, do something wrong, and you've blocked the pipe. Nevertheless, I decided it was a good enough benchmark. I finished up, held my breath, crossed my fingers, and turned the water back on. Then I went to look. And it wasn't leaking! And water was getting through! Maybe I could pull this off after all.

Tales from a Hostel at the Edge of the World

Except that the next two pipes were horses of a different color entirely. These were located underneath the main building, with heavy emphasis on the word *underneath*. They were at the end of a very long crawlspace, accessible only through a trap door in the floor of the living room. I had about three and a half feet to work with between the ground and the floor, or should I say, the mud and the floor, and in order to reach them I had to crawl under other pipes. Anyway, once I got to them I had more than enough room to work with and I tackled the first one. After finishing it up, I turned on the water, and presto: another success!

I called the mysterious off-island cabal that hired me to give them the update. Two out of three down, I reported. I had now run out of the supplies I needed, so I would go into town to provision in the morning and attempt the final one the next day. I was totally exhausted at this point. Then I hung up the phone and looked at the time. It was 4:30, which meant that I had just enough time to hop on my bike and get to the hardware store before it closed at 5:00. Off I went. What else was I going to do?

I got back and tackled the last pipe, managing to pull it off just as the sun was setting. I felt that the second pipe was better executed than the first and that the third pipe was better executed than the second. So this one would surely do the trick. I turned on the water, poked my head under the trapdoor, shined the flashlight, and discovered that I had actually managed to pull off all three pipes!

But still poking my head under the trapdoor, from a distance, I also discovered a fourth geyser, which lay just beyond what I had previously thought was the end of my solo plumbing career. This I was not expecting. I hadn't noticed it before, beyond the spray of the other pipes, but it was every bit as bad as the others. This one would surely have to wait until the next day, but I wasn't going to be daunted now. There may come a day, I thought to myself, when the armies of men lose their hope, lose their resolve, and choose to bow down to the armies of professional plumbers who refuse to plumb. But that day was not this day. Today we fought. And tomorrow we would ride again!

And then I ordered myself a pizza.

The next morning I descended once again to take a closer look at what lay before me, and it was much, much worse than I had thought. This one wasn't just a piece of pipe that had to be replaced. This was just above an L-shaped curve right above a drainage faucet, embedded within a busy network of other pipes about three inches away on either side. I had never done anything like this, and it wasn't at all clear how to even approach it. Which section to cut and replace? From where to where? And how? And here the plot thickens further, because at this stage of the journey the ground rises up. I now no longer had roughly three and a half feet to work with, but more like one and a half. I lay there dumbfounded. I stared and I thought. Was this even possible? I didn't think so.

And just then I noticed yet another hole in a pipe just beyond this one, in an even more inaccessible place. And then another just beyond that one! How many more might there be beyond that? Truth be told, I lost hope. I emerged into the daylight, and paced and ruminated, and then had another look. Nope, impossible. I went back a third time. Definitely impossible. I told Robert and Jenna and Nena the terrible news, and Jenna said, "Well, it doesn't sound so bad." And Bob said, "What else can you do but keep on?" Nena just smiled.

For this I would need new tools, so it was back off to the hardware store.

After that, once I started, it was all a blur. The details of the mechanics can't be described. It took hours and hours. It took thinking and rethinking. It took wedging myself into tiny spaces and coming to the realization that I was somehow a practitioner of yoga without ever having taken a class. It took using a blowtorch within three inches of other pipes and about five inches away from the wooden beams supporting the floor. It involved moments of intense anxiety and adrenaline rushes. There were times when my hands were literally shaking. The first three pipes had been a walk in the park compared to this. The last three pipes should have been impossible. I should not have been able to accomplish this task, and I'm not really sure if anyone should have. Somehow, at the end of the day, the task was accomplished. Without exaggerating, I felt like I couldn't even take credit for it. I was but a vessel. I still can't believe that it worked. I called Brad and told him that he wasn't going to believe that it worked either when he finally saw it. But somehow, what should have been impossible had been rendered possible.

And the water flowed.

The next question to face was why we still didn't have any *hot* water after all of this. And why there was steam coming from out of the boiler room where I had never seen it before. For this I was able to get some technicians to come by and take a look, and the answer was immediately forthcoming: the hot water heater was dead as a doorknocker. It had to be replaced entirely and there was no other option. They spent the entire next day removing the old one and installing the new one. At the end of the day, their last task was to turn it on to make sure that it was up to snuff. And it was. The only problem, they said, was that there was a major leak somewhere in the building. Until that was fixed they would have to keep it turned off.

I then murdered these men in cold blood and hid their bodies in the crawlspace. Not really. Actually, I double-checked everything I did and found it all intact. I then wandered around in a state of bewilderment for a while, until I remembered the trapdoor in the kitchen that I had been overlooking the entire time. I then poked my head underneath and, sure enough, there it was. The seventh pipe. The seventh leak.

This one might not be so bad, I thought. It wasn't too far from the trapdoor, I had a luxurious two-foot space to work with, and it seemed like a fairly straightforward job. The problem, which I discovered as soon as I cut the pipe, was that there was an unending trickle of water coming out of it. Every time I thought I had drained it completely, the trickle would return.

According to Newton's third law of plumbing, a pipe will take no solder whatsoever so long as it contains water. And I couldn't make the water disappear. My first bright idea was to test Newton's third law. It held. My second bright idea was to boil all the water out with the blowtorch. This didn't pan out either. After attempting a few other crafty schemes, I soon found myself at wit's end. This pipe wasn't supposed to be impossible, so why was it being so bloody impossible? Expletive!

I called Brad again. "What's the deal?" I asked. "There have to be some tricks to the trade here that I don't know about."

"Look," he said, "you know you can't do it with the water in there, so what are you going to do? First, you've got to let the air in somehow…"

"It's right underneath the faucets in the kitchen," I replied. "Should I open those?"

"Of course you open those! The next thing you do is… Look, just use your head, you take a piece of bread and you cram it in there…"

"Excuse me," I interjected, "Did you just say, 'a piece of bread'?"

"Of course. You take a piece of bread. Look, it's easily degradable. You cram it all the way in there. It absorbs the water. You get everything ready and once you put the bread in, you just do the job as quickly as you can before the water gets through."

I thanked Brad profusely. I knew that there had to be something I didn't know about. So I did as he suggested. And it worked.

Bread.

This bloody little pipe took longer than all of the others, but the work was finally done. We soon got the hot water heater up and running and everything else checked out. No less than five days after returning to the island, this particular saga had finally played itself out. As soon as I could, I took the most magnificent hot shower I've ever taken in all of my life. It was well earned and long overdue.

* * *

And at long last I was finally able to bask in the peace and serenity and the glow of the island. The multitude of stars at night was absolutely breathtaking, as was the nighttime roar of the ocean. The marsh to the west was alive with the chorus of spring peepers. I saw more rabbits scampering about than in previous years, and that was saying a lot. One afternoon a gorgeous neighboring cat came by and we bonded for some time. The next morning I saw her bounding across the yard with a dead bunny in her mouth, the huntress and her prey. There were seagulls aplenty, of course, but also lots of herons and hawks soaring about, while flocks of piping plovers dominated the beaches, dancing along the shore. The forest to the north had been ravaged by heavy winter snows, leaving many fallen trees in its wake. Fortunately, my two favorite trees were alive and intact, but many others that I loved didn't fare so well. But nature will rebound, as is her wont.

Chapter 17

Cimex lectularius

In which an ancient enemy returns to the hostel and battle is engaged.

The nature of this species appears to be such that it can sustain its ethereal existence only through a macabre ritual involving puncturing the skin and sucking the blood of a living host. Responding to warmth and carbon dioxide, the predator will quickly locate its prey. As with other blood-sucking creatures of the night, during feeding it will inject its anticoagulant saliva into its victim.

These predators tend not to live with humans and the only contact is the occasion of a blood feast. Most blood feeding occurs nocturnally, as they generally seek shelter during the day, becoming virtually lifeless during their sustained periods of digestion. However, contrary to common beliefs and superstitions, these opportunistic creatures can emerge and feed during the daylight, especially when underfed.

They can furthermore survive for long periods without feeding. And while their preferred host is human, they are also able to feed upon a wide variety of other warm-blooded animals, including rodents, rabbits and bats.

Being a cryptic species, they tend to seek shelter in a variety of dark locations, mostly close to mortal bedchambers. Given their mysterious, preternatural properties, they are able to hide under mattresses and floorboards and even behind paintings and carpets, as well as deep within the shadows of cracks and crevices of walls and bed frames.

These creatures tend to stay in close contact with each other and their presence can often be detected by a distinctively sweet, sickly smell. Blood spotting on mattresses and nearby furnishings is often the only sign that a visitation has occurred.

Jeff Becan

Cimex lectularius are great travelers of the world. And unbeknownst to most mortals, they have a worldwide network of distribution.

*   *   *

The preceding is a description of a diabolical species commonly referred to as *bedbugs*, paraphrased from a website by the Department of Medical Entomology at Westmead Hospital in New South Wales, Australia. Certain artistic liberties may have been taken. The Latin nomenclature literally means *bug of the bed*.

Bedbugs had been an occasional but nagging problem at the hostel during my previous seasons, most notably in the women's dorm. In fact, we never really had any problems anyplace else. In the past, I had felt that I had done everything in my power to hunt them down, but to limited success. The exterminator always came once a month to spray each and every bed, but experience had proven that that only did so much. They would disappear for a little while and then return with a vengeance. Only particular chemicals could kill them and they hadn't been the kind that I was ever able to get my hands on. Apparently a good blast of really hot steam could also knock them dead, and the previous year I *was* able to get my hands on a steamer.

I tried the steamer and, verily enough, painstakingly attacking every bed in the women's dorm, I did find that power steaming targeted cracks and crevices would often yield dead bedbugs and molten blood. When all of the aforementioned precautions didn't work, I resorted to taking pins, needles and penknives to their desired locations, dragging them out of their lairs and staking them through their hearts. But no matter what I did, the problems were always mitigated but never entirely eliminated.

Furthermore, on previous occasions when a victim/guest would report a problem, I would always immediately inspect the bed and the sheets. If genuine nocturnal feeding had actually occurred, then there might be a streak or two of blood on the sheets and I might even drag out a pest or two from their hiding places.

So this year, upon returning to the hostel, and even while I was working on discovering my inner plumber, I also discovered that the problem of bedbugs remained. But specifically they remained in a new and unprecedented location: my own bed. The first couple of nights had been fine, but finally one morning I woke up to discover that my sheets were markedly covered with not one or two, but scores of tiny but telltale streaks of blood. Apparently, I had been savaged.

I was fine with this. First of all, it was karma. After all, under my watch, despite my best intentions and efforts, several guests had become victims. It was only fair that I should share in their pain. Secondly, I welcomed the fact that I was alerted to this situation well before we opened. According to all the literature, *Cimex lectularius* are fairly temperate creatures, and cannot survive extremes of either high heat or freezing temperatures. Once again, the island had just undergone another extremely bitter winter, and yet these intractable creatures had somehow managed to survive. It was good to be aware of this now.

My equanimity was further aided by the fact that different people have different reactions to these things. Some people display small, well-defined red welts where they have been bitten. Some people produce swollen, bulbous cysts, and others just don't react much at all. Apparently I was of the latter variety. According to my sheets, I had been viciously attacked, but physiologically I had absolutely no reactions. No bumps, no itching, nothing. I suppose that also made things a little bit easier to take.

In any case, this time I did the same thing that I always did. I immediately washed the sheets on high heat and proceeded to inspect the bed. But this time, instead of finding one or two of these little beasties, which are about the size and shape of your average, garden-variety tick, I actually found an entire colony. Just beneath my mattress was a large, supportive piece of plywood. It was covered with them. I stopped counting when I reached fifty. My bed had become an ecosystem unto itself.

Nature will rebound, as is her wont.

I promptly took the plywood to my worktable, lit my blowtorch, and declared open season. After the ensuing bloodbath, I had both the plywood and the mattress hauled off to the dump. Every inch of the bed frame, every crack and crevice, was then thoroughly steamed, wiped down with a mixture of cleaning solution and rubbing alcohol (this doesn't kill them, but apparently it does irritate them, which counts for something), and then I used the only real tool I had in my arsenal, which was a chemical foam agent that, again, doesn't kill them, but does somehow prevent them from reproducing. Better than nothing, and one always has to use every tool one has at one's disposal.

Jeff Becan

Using my own bedchamber as a barometer of potential activity, I would eventually do the same thing to every single bed on the premises. With such a formidable adversary, there would be no punches pulled. Naturally, I called in the exterminator as well, but there would be a number of days before he could arrive. In the meantime, my supervisors had been alerted and, at long last, they were finally able to get me the lethal chemicals I needed that I could apply myself. The ammunition was ordered and on the way.

After the precautions I had already taken, I replaced my sheets and the next night was fine. I woke up in the morning and the sheets were spotless. The morning after, however, showed just how resilient these nosferatu actually were. Just a couple of splotches this time, but once again, the problem had been mitigated but not eliminated. So I repeated everything. The next morning the sheets were spotless. The following morning, however...

We repeated this little dance for some time until I finally noticed something crucial. As I was thoroughly steaming my bed frame for the umpteenth time, I happened to notice, almost out of the corner of my eye, two of the little beasties crawling on the baseboard heating unit right behind my bed. I staked them immediately and then finally put two and two together.

How could the answer have eluded me for so long? The only places in the entire complex where we had had outbreaks of bedbugs had been the women's dorm and now the Pequod. And the only places in the entire complex where we had baseboard heating units were the women's dorm and the Pequod.

I grabbed the steamer and would eventually spend hours upon hours meticulously clearing out about a decade's worth of dust and debris from every single baseboard heating unit. Once that was done, I went to town on them with all of my fancy chemicals. (For the record, these included Suspend ® SC liquid insecticide and DeltaDust ® powder insecticide, both made by a company called Bayer Environmental Science, followed by Gentrol ® Aerosol, Insect Growth Regulator.)

Fortunately I was able to do all of this before we opened. And after we opened we didn't have a single incident. It all added up. Bedbugs weren't supposed to be able to survive freezing temperatures, but if there remained just enough residual heat in the electric baseboards then that's where they could hide. That, plus the natural insulation of so much dust and debris, meant that they had not only been able to survive the winters, but they had probably also been quite comfortable. Previously we had spent all of our resources attacking the beds - the battlegrounds - but we had been completely unaware that their headquarters lay just beneath our feet.

My heart told me that, at long last, I had finally won this war. At the same time, I also knew my enemy far too well to let my guard down. I understood their motivations and tactics, and you might even say that I had developed a sort of respect for them. I therefore remained ever vigilant, and the garlic wreaths remained hung on their posts.

Chapter 18

The Story So Far

In which personalities clash and worlds collide - but all's well that ends well.

After fixing all the pipes and slaying all the vampires it was time to get to work on putting everything else in order. There was a lot of work that needed to get done, so I was glad when Arthur finally showed up. I had met Arthur two years ago and we had become fairly good friends. He stayed with us at the beginning of the season, then found work and housing and moved on, but we kept in touch. Later on in the season his housing fell through, and he returned to the hostel to see if I could be of some assistance. I needed lots of extra help at the time, he needed housing, and so we came to an arrangement. He primarily helped me with the cleaning and he did an exceptionally good job. I also just found him to be a pleasant and agreeable guy, and so I was convinced that he would make an ideal colleague this season.

So Arthur arrived in time to help get things in shape, and not a moment too soon. There was a lot to do and not much time now before we opened. And fortunately he wasn't the only help I had. The hostel had already become so busy that we had guests even before we opened, eight Bulgarians to be precise. Eva had stayed with us the previous season, so when she showed up unannounced with seven of her friends, I immediately gave them all a free place to stay and put them to work. It worked out well for everyone.

Eventually, everything got done, the place looked great, and we were ready to open. One of the last things to attend to was the light in the cupola. During the most recent renovations the lighting fixture had been removed but not replaced, and it was a good day when I finally found the time to replace it with another new one. That evening the light in the tower was shining once again, a signal to the world that the state of the hostel was good.

So the hostel was open, phase one had begun, when the vast majority of our guests were generally fun kids coming to the island to look for seasonal work and housing, and we were already busy. The reservation book was quickly filling up for the whole season and we were off to a great start.

Jeff Becan

And soon the problems with Arthur began to arise. I had had a few minor bumps with him already. There had been times when I had given him a few directions, which I felt he had turned into personal conflict. He was a little bit stubborn and a little bit feisty, but no big deal. I could deal with those things myself. The bigger problems were the complaints I was getting about him from other people. He was rubbing guests the wrong way, right and left, and I was hearing about it more and more. I was even getting complaints from people that he had only dealt with over the phone. To my surprise and dismay, his manner could be extremely abrupt and officious, not exactly ideal qualities in the world of hospitality. To put it simply, he just wasn't a 'people person'. He *could* be if he happened to like the people he was dealing with, but they seemed to be few and far between. The situation was quickly turning sour.

And then came Norinne, Dorothy and Michelle, three lasses from Ireland who were among the most colorful characters I had yet encountered. Whirlwinds of energy, they almost had to be experienced to be believed. The best way to describe them would be to say that each one was a rock star in her own right, and that all together they were a veritable hard-core rock and roll band, with all three members constantly bouncing off of each other as they performed. And although they weren't literally actually rock stars in real life, they *would* constantly break into song. Any casual word or phrase used in conversation could kick off a tune. One would start and the others would join in, anything from classics to pop songs to Broadway standards, whatever happened to fit the bill in their collective stream of consciousness. Furthermore, the language they used would make a sailor blush, as they constantly and unconsciously flowered every sentence with strings of well-placed expletives, delivered in the most enchanting, lilting brogues you've ever heard.

Somehow these three girls were an absolute delight. But like the Morrigan, the three-headed goddess from ancient Celtic mythology, they could also be a holy terror. Most of the problems would occur after the girls would return to the hostel in the wee hours of the morning, '*polluted* drunk', as Norinne would describe it, singing and emphasizing every syllable in the word with an hysterical, gleeful grin across her face. Whenever I would get complaints about them I would always take them aside and have a word with them and they were always profusely apologetic. As I explained to many people afterwards, they were quite possibly the worst guests we had ever had as well as possibly my favorites!

But one night was worse than the others. We happened to have a large group of fairly strait-laced, middle-aged women staying with us, many of whom just weren't particularly well suited to hostelling in the first place. On this particular occasion, the Morrigan returned home to the women's dorm, *polluted* drunk, at around 3am. According to the complaints I received from the other women, they were singing at the top of their lungs, and were apparently unable to stop even after they were asked to quiet down. To my disbelief, I was furthermore told that they were smoking in the women's dorm.

I had learned over the years that the manager is responsible for anything and everything anyone at the hostel says or does, so I had a lot of cleaning up to do. A lot of diplomacy and apologies to deliver to everyone who had complaints, and the assurance that I would do everything in my power to make sure that it wouldn't happen again. Interestingly enough, almost everyone who complained to me also added that no matter how upset they had been, they also found it impossible not to like the girls, whom they otherwise found quite charming and amusing, in their own fashion.

Not so with Arthur. Arthur may not have gotten along well with everyone, but it was abundantly clear that he absolutely *loathed* Norinne, Dorothy and Michelle. It was almost pure hatred that seethed from his very being whenever they were around, creating an atmosphere behind the desk that I felt could only be described as poisonous. Working in this kind of environment really required one to be able to get along with all kinds of people and to be able to rise to all types of social challenges. Arthur was failing on all of these counts.

But in the meantime, I had the girls to attend to. I sat them down and we had a serious talk. I told them what I had heard from the other women, and none of them could believe it. In their recollection they had come home so polluted drunk that they all passed out immediately upon hitting the bed. And as for the allegations of smoking, they denied it vehemently. They couldn't imagine doing such a thing. I told them that I couldn't imagine them doing such a thing either, but that I could easily imagine them being so polluted that they might not be able to remember the ruckus they caused before passing out. Eventually, they agreed to this possibility as well.

And as the memories of the night began to reemerge into the daylight, Michelle even remembered Dorothy talking in her sleep, saying something about putting out a cigarette. Dorothy then recalled this too. She remembered having a dream in which the other girls were smoking and she was telling them repeatedly, *Put out that cigarette, Put out that cigarette!* It seemed entirely possible to them (and to me) that someone overhearing Dorothy shouting this drunkenly in her sleep, and especially after all the other commotion in the middle of the night, could have easily believed that they were smoking in the dorm when they actually weren't.

Regardless, I delivered my sentence, which was nothing less than exile. Nor and Dor and Michelle had been staying in the women's dorm for some time now, and they obviously felt quite at home there, but after this incident I told them that I wanted them to transfer to the co-ed dorm in the back building. It was a smaller dorm with fewer people and, if nothing else, if anything similar were to happen again, then at least it wouldn't happen to the same women in the women's dorm. They were all terribly disappointed about this, but at the same time they also completely understood my perspective, and they were more than willing to oblige.

After this judgment was meted, all was well in the kingdom. The strait-laced women had seen what I had done and had appreciated the gesture. The girls apologized to them, their apologies were accepted, and everyone got along swimmingly thereafter.

Everyone, that is, except for Arthur, who apparently decided that he could no longer speak to the Irish girls, let alone make eye contact with them. The girls were baffled. They would tell him 'good morning' upon greeting him, and he would pretend that they weren't even there. After this incredibly bizarre, childish and completely unacceptable behavior continued, Michelle decided to apologize directly to Arthur for their behavior. He curtly told her that he didn't accept her apology.

When I heard about this, it was the last straw. Arthur's poisonous behavior was out of control, and I was becoming more and more furious with him. As difficult as it was to appease the women and handle the girls that morning, dealing with Arthur's temperament was even worse. It seemed to me that he was not only unfit for this kind of work, but that he was also not even happy here.

So we talked. I told him my perspective, which was that all things considered, I didn't think that the situation was working out and that I had a hard time imagining it improving in the future. His reaction was instinctive and combative and a shouting match quickly ensued. We were both making our points, but we were both getting more and more frustrated. When we started arguing in circles I just decided to put an end to it. I told him that we were repeating ourselves, we weren't getting anywhere, we were both frustrated with each other, and that we would put this down for the time being and take it up again later. He accepted this and we parted company.

That night I noticed that the light in the cupola had been turned off. I decided it would remain off.

I was still furious, and I wasn't used to being furious. I was somewhat surprised that Arthur was fighting to keep his position, as I had perceived him to be so miserable, but I chalked this up to pride rather than genuine commitment to the job. So I decided to come up with a list of conditions that he would have to agree to if he really wished to remain. It was clear and to the point and also perfectly reasonable. The central theme was civility.

The next day we sat down again. The air had cleared a little. I shared my perspective, handed him my list, and we both went over it together item by item. Our meeting was short. He swallowed his pride, quickly agreed to all of the terms, and accepted that any further violations would result in termination. To a certain extent I felt that my initial attempt to get rid of him had failed markedly, but at the same time I also felt that this was fair. Everyone deserves a second chance. Or whatever number we were at by now.

In the meantime, I desperately needed additional staff. This season had been so much busier than the previous seasons, and had taken off so much faster, and I found myself increasingly overextended. Fortunately, we had two young women staying with us, about whom I had a great feeling from the moment they arrived. Laura and Mary were best friends who had just graduated college together, and they had come to the island, along with most of our other phase-one guests, to look for work and housing.

I decided early on that I wasn't going to advertise any open positions but would rather just surreptitiously keep my eye out for candidates who I felt had the right stuff. Weeks had now passed and no one had really inspired much confidence in me until Mary and Laura arrived. They were both charming and personable, they were able to get along with all types, and they were clearly bright.

Jeff Becan

I had already decided to take them aside to talk to them about this possibility, but before I even had the opportunity, Laura asked me if there were any open positions at the hostel! The three of us sat down to talk, and we all emerged with beaming smiles on our faces. They started working immediately and they quickly picked up on everything. We soon became fast friends as well as colleagues, and we were all just as pleased as punch.

Well not all of us.

As noted, Arthur didn't seem to get along with too many people and Mary and Laura were no exceptions. He tolerated them, but clearly felt threatened by their presence, and was no doubt threatened as well by the fact that they had learned the ropes so much faster than he did. I also began to perceive the impression that he was lording a sense of superiority over them, most likely to compensate for feelings of inferiority, and my suspicions were soon proved correct. Laura and Mary eventually and reluctantly came to me to express frustrations that they had been trying to keep under wraps. Apparently the impressions I perceived were even worse than I imagined.

I had yet another talk with Arthur, and without even mentioning anything that the girls had told me in confidence, I did impress upon him the fact that he and Mary and Laura were all part of the same team and that, as far as I was concerned, all were equals and should be treated accordingly. This seemed well received at the time, but it made no difference in the end.

At the end of her shift one night Mary had been attempting to clean the kitchen. Arthur was also in the kitchen, bantering around with a few of the select guests that he happened to like. Rather than moving out of her way to let her clean, he stayed right where he was and, in the course of his continued bantering, Mary felt that he was openly mocking her in front of his audience. She told me this the next day and she was actually visibly shaken. Normally positive and easygoing, Mary was clearly upset, which made me furious, yet again…

The next day I told Arthur that I felt he owed her an apology. He was astonished and claimed that he was just joking around with her, giving me a lengthy play by play of the previous night's events, all of which just seemed to support the details that Mary had shared with me. My perspective, I explained to him, was that if you hurt someone's feelings to such an extent, you owe them an apology whether you intended to hurt them or not. He told me he would speak to them both and he asked me to give him my trust that he would handle the situation appropriately. I told him that this was a good move and that if he asked me for my trust I would gladly give it to him.

He blew it.

He did sit down to have a talk with them, but when they came to see me afterwards they were practically trembling. He delivered no apology, but defended his behavior once again, he told them he had no interest in being friends with them but would endeavor to treat them in a professional manner, and he went on to lay down a number of rules for the professional behavior he expected from them. He then continued by saying some not-so-flattering things about yours truly, which he told them not to repeat to me. Mary and Laura were stunned. Of course they came to me.

Enough was really quite enough at this point. I didn't have to take much time to think things over before I confronted Arthur and told him that the climate he had created was intolerable, that the situation was untenable, and that the road had finally come to an end. I told him that I naturally found it regrettable, but at the same time that was my final answer. I was clear and firm and he accepted my decision accordingly.

So there I was, third season, third head on the chopping block. A whole lot of no fun, but the best interests of the hostel had to come first.

In an attempt to make things less awkward for Arthur, I decided not to tell Mary and Laura until he was gone. As it happened he chose not to speak to them from that point on anyway. Even so, the next couple of days weren't as awkward as they could have been. The situation was so clear-cut that there was really nothing left to argue about. Arthur quietly prepared to leave and everything was extremely civil, at least between the two of us.

And on the morning he departed we actually had a nice conversation, and for that moment in time he seemed like the old Arthur I once knew, Arthur the friend. And I have to give him credit for that. It was a difficult and trying situation for both of us, to say the least, but we discussed matters open and cordially. In closing, I told him that, you never know, this might even be something that our friendship could survive. He accepted this as well. Soon thereafter his cab arrived, we exchanged a friendly hug, and he was off.

Thus passes Arthur, I thought to myself. And thus ended this particularly long and drawn-out saga. It was the end of an era and the beginning of a new one. And no matter how dark those days had been, the fog would soon lift, and much happier days were soon to follow.

Chapter 19

Halcyon Days

In which sometimes the universe conspires in one's favor.

As bleak as the early part of the season had been, the skies soon opened and the climate that emerged was quickly becoming as warm, positive and lovely as it had ever been. I felt like we were not only back on track to being the best damn hostel in the country, but possibly the best in the universe! I also felt that we were creating a veritable community that was more like one big, happy extended family.

The phase one seasonal workers came in droves and, this year, housing was especially difficult to find. And although the hostel wasn't meant for long-term accommodation, for a number of people it essentially became just that. I think that there were two factors involved. One was that housing *was* especially difficult to find, but the other was that so many people felt so comfortable at the hostel that they didn't want to leave!

But leave they would soon have to. Phase two of the season was prime time, when we had loads of big group reservations that were pretty much booked back-to-back. For July and August these groups made up the bulk of our clientele, but we would still have a lot of travelers and vacationers as well. Moreover, this season the numbers were off the charts. We were busier than ever and the hostel had been booked solid, if not overbooked, most of the time.

The problems thus came when phases one and two collided. Most of the phase one seasonal workers eventually found housing after many weeks of searching, but not everyone, and there were many weekends when our day-to-day and week-to-week lodgers had to be sent into exile because of large group reservations that had been made well in advance. I made sure that everyone knew the drill and we always got full cooperation, but that didn't always make it any easier.

One particular occasion stood out. We had three great kids staying with us at the time. Nick and Jake and Matt struck me as a little rough around the edges at first, but it soon became clear that they were actually great guys and friends since childhood. They had been staying with us for some time and all was well, but then they had to find someplace else to stay on a night when we were booked solid.

That night Jake ended up in the emergency room because he had gone out to the bars, drank more than he could handle, and he ended up in a bike accident that scratched up his face, earned him ten stitches across his forehead and dislocated his shoulder. I told his mother over the phone that it was the one night when he was out from under our wing and that that was what happened! He had previously been working on a construction crew but he had to take a leave of absence after the accident, so the hostel became a convalescence home for him during his recovery. It was a dramatic episode, but his recovery was fairly swift, and it felt good to be of support to him. Nick and Jake and Matt eventually found housing, but they stayed in touch and would of course come back to visit from time to time.

Simon and Pavel were two guys from Bulgaria who eventually became the stuff of legend in their search for housing. I think they struggled harder than anyone else. I had told them the same thing I told everyone, which was that the best way to find housing was to get out on the streets and talk to as many people as possible. It was mostly found through word of mouth. Whenever they weren't working their jobs they did just that. They dressed up in their Sunday best and went into town and talked to everyone they could.

And each day they came back more and more dejected and down on their luck. Finally they tried something that no one else had the guts to try. They spent an entire day sitting outside the grocery store holding up signs advertising that they were in search of housing. By the end of the day they had three leads and they ended up in a great place for just the two of them with every possible amenity and at an excellent price. They were elated that their hard work and perseverance paid off. We were all sad the day they moved out, but they did well for themselves and they also came back to visit often.

Now I had a new piece of advice for people searching for housing, but Nandra was the only other one brave enough to try it. Nandra was a totally cool hippie chick from Florida who liked to bounce around the world, always looking for new experiences and making the most out of life. Just a little bit older than the rest, she was also a bit wiser, and totally comfortable in her own skin. She was a true original, a unique woman with a unique look.

Tales from a Hostel at the Edge of the World

She not only sported the funkiest outfits, but she had one of the coolest haircuts I had ever seen: dark brown shoulder length hair and bangs, but with a shaved band across the middle that she dyed with different colors and different patterns from week to week, anything from pink and blue stripes to leopard spots. In addition to being super-cool, she was also just an awesome human being.

Nandra's repeated attempts advertising herself outside the grocery store didn't yield her housing right away. But she kept at it and for a time she became known around the island as 'the housing lady'! People she didn't know would stop her in the street to ask her if she had found anything yet. Eventually she landed a restaurant job that came with housing. She already had another job that she loved and she wasn't too thrilled about the restaurant gig, but she took it for the housing that came with it. By that time she had become completely ingratiated into our hostel family and it was a tragic day for everyone when she moved out.

But Nandra would come back at least once a week to cook dinner for me and Mary and Laura and anyone else who might show up, so we were always kept abreast of the continuing developments in her life. We knew that she hadn't been happy at the restaurant and had considered the option of quitting, but out of a sense of responsibility she couldn't quite get herself to do it. Then came the happy day: Due to lack of business, the restaurant decided to let her go. I told her that I thought that sometimes the universe conspires in one's favor and that, as far as I was concerned, she could break a precedent and stay with us for the rest of the season. We were all delighted.

One night while working the front desk I received a phone call from a woman named Fortune, who sounded like she was in dire straights. She pleadingly asked me if we had any availability that night and we did. I gave her directions and told her to come straight away. Later that night the phone rang again. She had made it to our street but she wasn't sure where we were. "I think I'm on your front porch," she told me.

I put the phone down and ran to the entrance but she wasn't there. She was obviously in the neighborhood though, so I told her that I would come down the street with a flashlight to find her. It was a dark foggy night so the flashlight lit up the air like a beam. When she saw it from the end of the road, she was so happy. "Thank God!" she cried, "You're like a beacon of light!" She would eventually tell everyone that I was her guardian angel. And I was.

Jeff Becan

Fortune was older but very young at heart. She hailed from Hawaii and was one of the funniest and most endearing women I have ever had the pleasure to know. Everyone loved her and so it wasn't much of a surprise that she soon became fast friends with Nor, Dor and Michelle. Eventually the four of them found housing together, and it happened to be just down the street, which was great. Since we were all neighbors now, we still got to hang out all the time, and I no longer had to worry about the Morrigan. It was the best of all possible worlds.

It didn't last forever though. Their housing eventually fell through when their landlord erupted into one too many psychotic episodes. But by that time the Irish girls had found a sugar daddy, a computer billionaire with a spacious flat in Manhattan as well as a huge house on the island. He liked them so much that he would fly them to New York on the weekends aboard his private jet. He actually seemed to be a decent guy and they took to him as much as he took to them. Purely out of his fondness for them, after they moved out of their house, he told them they could stay at his place for free and for as long as they liked. They happily accepted.

Being in a somewhat different position in life, Fortune preferred to come back to the hostel and, as her guardian angel, I was more than happy to take her back in. The only problem, she told me over the phone, was that she had now acquired a new puppy and she knew that I probably wouldn't want it to sleep in the hostel. This was true, I told her. Pets weren't allowed in the hostel. There were too many people out there with allergies or other issues so that wouldn't work out at all. The puppy would have to stay with me.

Bodhi was about twelve months old, mostly yellow lab with a little bit of cocker spaniel in him, and he was adorable. The arrangement that we came to was that Fortune was the mother and I was the godfather. He essentially became the hostel dog and was a huge hit with everyone, but especially with the camp kids, who just fawned all over him. He was so well suited to the hostel that the only problem was that we spoiled him to pieces.

Fortune was a big hit with everyone too. She became something of the hostel mom and was a tremendous help to us, constantly cleaning the kitchen, sweeping the floor, and attending to laundry, purely out of the goodness of her heart and her love for the hostel. She would collect Bodhi early every morning to take care of him and I became so used to it that after a while I could sleep soundly through her visits, even when she was cleaning my kitchen!

Tales from a Hostel at the Edge of the World

Fortune was so lovable and quirky that she could furthermore somehow get away with telling young camp kids things like, "I hope you're going to put those fucking dishes away!" We were constantly entertained by her stories, such as the adventure she had when she accidentally gave away her deceased father's ashes to someone and then managed to get them back. Or the story about the housing that she almost took before she found out that the landlady had murdered four of her previous husbands and was known around the island as the Black Widow. Fortune was a gem. She was wonderful to have around and, as far as I was concerned, she could stay with us for the rest of the season as well - and her little dog too!

Then there was Vish and Ciaran. Vish was an American kid who went to art school in Glasgow and spent his summers working on the island. The best words to describe him would have to have been 'unbridled enthusiasm'. He was hilarious and his favorite word when describing people, places, things and events was always '*amazing*'! Ciaran, as the name might suggest, was our resident leprechaun. He was from Dublin and was totally great as well, with a sense of humor and facial expressions that reminded many people of Robin Williams.

With most of our phase one people, after too many days of staying at the hostel, I would do my best to encourage them, to *nudge* them, if you will, to do their best to find housing. Not so with Vish and Ciaran. They were in no hurry to leave and we were in no hurry to get rid of them. Their mirth and enthusiasm were great elements to have around, they got along terrifically with everyone, and everyone loved them.

And then, much to everyone's surprise, after about five weeks of staying with us, the day finally came when they told us that they had found housing and they moved out. Just like that. We were all dumbfounded. It was a heartfelt goodbye and, even though we knew they'd come back often, the hostel just didn't seem the same without them.

Two days later they both came back! They were miserable with their new arrangement and they missed the hostel. I told them that they were absolutely welcome back and that we would do everything in our power to accommodate them. But it might mean that on some nights they would have to sleep in a storage closet. They both agreed to this immediately.

"Actually," Vish mused, "sleeping in a storage closet would be *amazing*!"

But the next good development was that I would soon have a new part-time employee for a month in the form of my old friend, Susan! She and I always stayed in touch and, earlier in the season, when she knew that I was on the lookout for additional employees, she had volunteered herself. I was delighted to make it happen, and this meant we would also get to have Anne and Charlie as part of the package! I loved all three of them and it was great to have them all on board and officially part of the family.

One particular day there came a sublime and beautiful moment that just seemed to sum everything up for me. It was around midday and I was running around inventorying the beds, double-checking the reservations for the day, and just taking care of business. Mary was sitting outside at one of the picnic tables, visiting with her mother and her two brothers who had come to visit. Laura was cleaning in the women's dorm, Anne was mopping the dining room floor, and Susan and Charlie were folding blankets in the back building. Meanwhile, Bodhi was happily playing outside in the yard while Fortune was doing our laundry. With all hands on deck the entire complex was cleaned up and in perfect shape in record time. The state of the hostel had never been better.

I remain firmly convinced that sometimes the universe conspires in one's favor. Later that night, after a spectacular sunset, the stars were shining, the waves were crashing, a full moon lit up the night and I felt truly blessed.

Chapter 20

The Other Side

In which a bridge is built between the worlds and astonishing answers are revealed.

As the nucleus of the hostel family, Laura and Mary and I made for a fantastic team and we were also great friends. Most nights when the workday was done, we would gather in the Pequod, put on some music, have a few beers and just enjoy each other's company. In the course of time, I ended up telling them some of my spooky stories from the previous seasons. Not only were they intrigued, but it turned out that Mary had had more than her fair share of paranormal experiences as well.

Before coming to the island, some very strange things had occurred at Mary's home. And for whatever reason, the incidents that she described would only happen when she was visiting her mother and brothers on breaks from college. Eventually, the entire family became convinced that they were being haunted by the spirits of Mary's deceased grandparents.

On one occasion, Mary's mother was busy doing chores around the house when she heard the voice of her deceased father behind her. She quickly turned around to find no one there. On another occasion, someone had heard some distinct noises coming from the attic. They soon went to investigate, only to discover that some old boxes of family photographs had been opened and that various photos had been taken out and arranged in deliberate patterns all over the floor. On a third occasion, strange noises had been heard coming from one of the bedrooms. Inside this bedroom there were two framed photographs hanging on the wall, one was a picture of Mary and the other was of one her brothers. When they opened the door, both pictures were dramatically swinging on the wall from side to side.

Because of such bizarre experiences, Mary was quite open to the idea of the Ouija board. Ironically, although Laura was initially a little more guarded, it soon became clear that, of the three of us, Laura was the strongest medium. As for myself, I wasn't necessarily closed to anything, and I certainly believed Mary's stories, especially after her mother confirmed them all for me. However, when it came to the Ouija board I remained convinced that it was a fun parlor game and not necessarily much more.

That said, once the three of us started playing, there were many occasions when the stories that came through felt so real that it was as difficult to disbelieve them in my heart as it was to believe them in my head.

One night Mary and Laura were on the board while I was asking questions and writing everything down. The 'spirit' with whom we were communicating initially identified herself as Marie, and she began by telling us that there were lost souls trapped on the island that needed to move on. We asked how many, and at first it seemed to us that the answer was six. Marie then corrected us by telling us that there were six thousand! Then she mentioned the arch.

I wasn't sure what she meant by this and so I asked. However, we were now talking to someone else, someone named Helen. Helen told us that she wanted to pass through the arch but that Marie would have to stay. We asked why and the answer was that no spirit would be able to pass without Marie. Marie was described as a sort of spiritual midwife, helping good people pass through this mysterious arch so that they could pass on to the other side.

I asked Helen how she died and she answered that what had killed her was 'a coat hanger'. She had died in an abortion clinic. 'Not good to be pronounced dead upon arrival,' she informed us. After giving us a few more details about where and when, she finally told us that she had been killed by a man on the island, and that she believed that only a man on the island could now release her. I asked how this could be done. 'Through an arch,' came the answer.

Then Marie returned. 'This is no dream', she informed. 'Make an arch.' We asked who should make an arch.

'The manager,' she answered.

I told her that I was willing to do this, but that I thought the concept of a gateway was potentially one that could work in either direction. I wanted assurance that any such arch would only be used for good people and for good purposes. She then gave me this assurance and all I could do was accept it. Finally I asked why they actually needed a physical arch. The answer: 'An arch allows a mourning of the soul.'

Who was I to argue? It was one thing to logically declare that anything that came through on the board could be entirely explained by subconscious mental activity. It was another thing to actually believe that.

Tales from a Hostel at the Edge of the World

So the next day I set about my task. I found some suitable material in the tool shed and then I found a suitable spot. There was a semi-hidden path that ran from the hostel grounds down to the salt marsh. Midway along this path I erected my arch, fashioned with two wooden poles and half of a bicycle tire, and adorned with decorative greenery. It was large enough for anyone to walk through, and upon setting it up I declared a benediction to clarify the intentions. The arch would stand as a symbol of mourning for those who had passed, and a portal through which only good, truthful, but otherwise lost souls could now pass on. No evil was to come of it. I prayed over it and there it stood for several weeks, until the end of the season when I felt that it was finally time to take it down.

* * *

The next tale to come through for us was so astonishing that it was even more difficult to disbelieve. The entire session was long and drawn out and actually took place over three consecutive nights. This was something I had never witnessed before.

On the first night, the first name to come through was Agatha. Then came the name Mack. We asked for a last name, but there was no answer. Then came the word, 'Mama', followed by a question: 'Am I dead?'

"Is this Mack or Agatha?" we asked. It was Agatha. She told us that she was born in 1817 and died in 1839, which would have made her twenty-two. 'I am dead,' she declared.

Mack then returned and his story began to emerge. He lived on the island but he couldn't tell us how he died. He was only two years old. He was not happy where he was and someone else was with him.

'Goodbye.' The planchette then moved off the board, thus ending the first session.

On the second night, Agatha returned. 'I am dead,' she declared once again. She then told us that her middle name was Nelly and that her last name was Brown. Agatha Nelly Brown. Mack then returned and spelled his name twice.

Agatha, who had lived on the island and died on the island, told us that she didn't know where she was right now. She told us exactly where she lived when she was alive, but she informed us that she didn't know where she was buried.

'Sad mom,' she said.

Mack returned. 'Mack not Agatha. Mack not Agatha. I am dead.' Mack then told us that he didn't know where their mother was. He told us that he and Agatha were brother and sister and that she was older. Moreover, he told us that Agatha knew where Mama was but wouldn't tell him. We asked why, and Agatha told us that she was trying to protect him.

'I am dead,' she then reiterated. Furthermore, 'I was bad. I am near.'

"How did you die?" we asked.

'Dad. Dad killed Mack. Dad was crazy. Dad was mean.'

"What did your Dad do?"

'He knocked down trees for a living. He was a lumberjack. Mama was a housewife. Dad killed them. Mama was there but didn't do anything.'

The planchette then moved off the board, thus ending the second session.

The third night began with an imperative: 'Question Samantha.'

"What do you mean?" we asked. "Who is Samantha?"

'Mama was nice and good,' Agatha told us.

But, said Mack, 'A mean father. Not a man to make mad. Make me dead by knocking a mallet against my head.'

"What can we do to help?"

'Find my Mama.' How? 'Samantha Mather. Another sister. Make her meet me here. Agatha Brown. Dead. Find Samantha. Talk to her.' How? 'On the board.'

We then asked for Samantha and she came through loud and clear. She told us that she had moved on to Heaven but that Agatha and Mack had not. We told her that Agatha and Mack were not happy, that they wanted to move on but that they couldn't for some reason. We wanted to help them and they asked for you, Samantha. They felt that there was some way that Samantha could help, perhaps by disclosing the whereabouts of their mother.

Samantha then responded, 'Agatha is a Mama. Mack is my nephew. Agatha is his mother. Mack is her son and her brother. Mack is my brother and nephew.'

It took the three of us a minute to comprehend this and then the realization hit us like a ton of bricks.

"Who knew about this?" we asked.

'My mother. My father killed her. Dad killed his wife, Agatha and Mack.'

"Is there anything else you want to tell us?"

'No,' she said. And then she was gone.

Mack and Agatha then reemerged. They wanted to know if we had found Samantha and we told them we had. Mack wanted to know what she said. This suddenly felt very somber. Laura and Mary looked at me. I took a deep breath. And then I told Mack everything that Samantha told us. We were all deeply sorry.

The first response was this, 'You are making me upset. I am sad. Go make him pay!' It was Mack.

Then there was a long pause. Finally, 'I am sad and happy.'

Another long pause. 'I am happy.'

"Agatha," we asked, "why didn't you tell Mack?"

'I am a mom,' she told us. Fair enough.

"Do you think you will both be able to move on now?" we asked.

This was followed by another long pause.

'I hope so.' Pause.

'Thank you. I am happy. Goodbye.'

And that was the last we ever heard from Mack or Agatha. The session was finally over. As intense as it was, we all felt that it couldn't have ended more successfully.

* * *

Some time later, Mary came to me and told me something I wasn't expecting. She had been thinking about it a while, she said, and she had decided that she wanted to see if she could communicate with her grandparents through the board.

I was reluctant about this, not because I was against the idea in principle, but rather because I didn't want to see her disappointed. I told her that I had actually witnessed many Ouija board sessions in the past in which people had specifically asked to speak to loved ones who had passed on, but that I had never seen any results. Generally, whoever seems to be coming through on the board is just what you get. No requests. Samantha Mather had been an extremely unusual exception.

But Mary wanted to try anyway. She wanted to know why the spirits of her grandparents still seemed to be lingering. She wanted to know what was wrong.

Jeff Becan

The first time we tried they came through for us immediately! I was astonished. Curiously, they told us that they had passed on to a better place and that they were both very happy, but they also confirmed that they had been responsible for the strange goings on at Mary's house. The first reason was simply that they felt that they had been forgotten and that they wanted the family to remember them. But they also had some very specific, very personal concerns about Mary and one of her brothers in particular. They described these concerns, which clearly resonated with Mary. Everything they communicated seemed to be valid and born out of love.

Mary and Laura had been on the board during all of this and I had been transcribing the session. After Mary felt that she understood what her grandparents wanted to tell her, she then asked for permission to ask some personal questions that could perhaps confirm that it was actually her grandparents that were communicating to her.

At this point I felt that if we really wanted confirmation then Mary shouldn't be on the board. Any further information that might come through could very well be coming from Mary herself, and so she and I switched places. With me and Laura on the board, Mary then began to ask a number of specific questions of her grandparents, some of which she knew the answers to, some of which she thought she knew the answers to, and some of which she simply didn't know the answers to. She asked them how they first met, where and when and how her grandfather proposed marriage to her grandmother, and where they had lived and worked. She asked them what their favorite pet had been, where they were when she was born, and questions about other members of their family.

All of the answers were immediately forthcoming, and everything that came through had been information that neither Laura nor I could have possibly known. Nevertheless, Mary was perplexed. Some of the answers had corresponded with what she had been expecting, or at least hoped to hear, but other answers left her confused. For example, they had given her specific addresses of places where they used to live that she had never heard of. They had also told her that she had been born in a particular hospital that wasn't the name of the hospital that Mary had been told. They told her that her grandfather had worked at a particular building in New York, but Mary knew that he had actually worked someplace else. And when telling her what their favorite pet had been they gave her a name that she had never heard before.

Tales from a Hostel at the Edge of the World

All told, Mary had probably asked about twenty questions of them, and wrote down all of the answers, but after such a mixed bag of responses she was no longer sure that any of it had been authentic. Her grandparents then closed the session with a message of love to pass on to Mary's family and then they left.

The next day Mary called her mother to talk about it and was shocked to discover that absolutely everything that had come through had been true. Her mother confirmed that they had in fact lived at the addresses given, that before her grandfather worked at the Empire State Building he had worked at the Chrysler building, and that Gus had been their favorite dog, who had died before Mary was born. She also learned that the hospital where she had been born had changed its name. At the time that Mary was born, it had in fact been called Lakeview, which was a name that Mary had never known. And everything else her grandparents had communicated, Mary's mother confirmed unequivocally. Not only was it all information that Laura and I could never have possibly known, but most of it was information that Mary herself never knew. Mary and her family took all of the messages to heart, and nothing spooky ever happened in their household again.

As for me, I was floored. If Mary's grandparents had been legitimate, then what about all the rest of it? Had there, in fact, been 'some truth behind all messages' after all? And if so, had we honestly helped thousands of lost souls pass through an arch and into a better reality? Had the truth really set Mack and Agatha free?

I think in our hearts, Mary and Laura and I believed.

Chapter 21

Starry Nights

In which the halcyon days of summer continue into the nights and life is good.

Back on this side of life, the halcyon days of summer continued. There were some days when the mood was so nice and warm that it felt like we were all living in an imaginary realm by the sea. Or a yellow submarine. Life remained beautiful.

My birthday soon came around and it was a blast. That afternoon, Susan, Anne and Charlie had beautifully decorated my place with colorful ribbons, and that evening we had a barbeque that quickly turned into a grand soiree. Fortune and Bodhi were there, Mary and Laura, Vish and Ciaran, all the usual suspects. We also had a lovely returning guest named Evelyn, with her son Alex and his friend Isaac. But then even more people arrived, including my old friend Alejandra, who brought her toy Chihuahua with her. So we had all ages, lots of nationalities, and no less than two dogs running around. We ate, drank and were merry well into the wee hours of the night.

And then three days later it was Susan's birthday so we did it all over again! This time I decorated for her. Susan's party started off a little more low-key than mine, but that soon changed as well, as the margaritas flowed and more and more people arrived. The last guests to arrive were a couple of our neighbors, Tom and Margaret, two endearingly clueless hippie kids from the house next door. (Between Tom and Bodhi, we weren't sure who was more intelligent.) Laura's theory was that Tom and Margaret were a couple by default, simply because they were the only people they could each remember. But they were sweet kids, they amused everyone to no end, and their quirky presence was a fun finale to the celebration.

The tide ebbed and flowed. By this time, as regards the Morrigan, the fellowship had been broken. Michelle had moved on to visit friends in Florida, while Nor and Dor had gone off to have adventures in San Francisco. Meanwhile, Ciaran had learned that he had failed an exam back home in Ireland, so he had to head back and take it over again in order to graduate. We threw him a nice farewell party too and hoped that he would return soon. And then even Fortune and Bodhi left us to go live on a boat that Fortune had somehow acquired in the course of her adventures. It wouldn't be the same without them.

So we had lost our hostel puppy, but we soon gained another one for a brief period of time. We had a really great group of guests staying with us from upstate New York. There were seven of them in all, but Natalie and James and their young son Ryan had just acquired a new puppy in the form of a Nova Scotia Duck Tolling Retriever. Quincy was his name and we all decided that he almost made up for Bodhi's absence. He was just five weeks old, extremely good-natured, with eyes and facial expressions that seemed almost human. He was a delightful little creature and I had as much fun bonding with him as I did with his crew of humans.

One afternoon, the clan was about to head into town and I had volunteered to take care of Quincy. Before their cab arrived, we were all sitting outside in the yard and I had taken one end of Quincy's leash and tied it to the beach chair I was sitting on. Later when I got up to take care of something, for some reason, Quincy became excitable and he leapt up and started running around, only to discover that he was being chased by a giant blue beach chair! This excited him still further and he ran as fast as he could, straight into the hostel, with the beach chair doggedly pursuing him every step of the way. It was quite a sight and we were all floored with laughter, even though poor Quincy was scared out of his wits. After I rescued him he led me immediately to the back porch of the far back building, as far away from the beach chair as we could possibly be. We sat down and decompressed after all the excitement and it probably took a good twenty minutes before his little heart rate went back to normal. Quite the adventure!

During the same time that the New York crowd was around, we also had another guest in the house called Alvin. Alvin was yet another certifiable lunatic. The problem with Alvin was that he would latch on to anyone he could find and start babbling incessantly about pure tedium. He was so bad and so crazy that the only way to make it stop would be to find a way to just get up and leave. Sometimes even that wouldn't work as he would just keep on talking whether or not he had an audience. We also observed him several times having very loud one-way conversations on his cell phone and none of us were convinced that there was anybody else on the other end. A strange bird, to say the least. Utterly harmless, but totally nuts.

Tales from a Hostel at the Edge of the World

So one night after closing down the office, Mary and Laura and I were hanging out in my place and, outside the screen door, we saw that Alvin had sucked James from New York into one of his conversations/monologues. The exchange had been going on for some time, and so we decided that we should try to rescue James from the situation. I came up with a plan, walked out towards Alvin and James, and then noticed that James actually seemed to be actively participating in the conversation. So I proceeded into the hostel and then thought I would attempt another rescue operation on the way back. Once again, I returned only to find James very much participating in the exchange. Fair enough, I thought.

The next day I asked James what in the world he was doing by willingly placing himself in such verbal entrapment, and he told me that he had been totally fascinated by what Alvin was talking about. Alvin's typical discourses generally involved excruciating details about vacations he had taken, the itinerary route he had taken to the hostel, or meals he had recently had or was planning for the following day. But this time James told me that Alvin had brought up the subject of the Heaven's Gate UFO cult that had committed mass suicide in California during the 90's. One might recall that their plan was to kill themselves in their sneakers and then magically wake up on the Mothership trailing Comet Hale-Bopp.

According to Alvin, Heaven's Gate had succeeded in doing just that! Furthermore, one of Alvin's uncles had been a member. But then the story got even better because Alvin himself was supposed to have gone with them. They had saved a space for him, but he had been running late and wasn't able to make it in time and so he missed the whole thing.

I was really sad when our New York crew had to leave, and everybody was sad to see Quincy leave. Curiously, no one was too heartbroken to see Alvin leave.

It had been wonderful to have Susan, Anne and Charlie with us for a whole month. In addition to all of the wild parties they were privy to, the four of us had lots of other great times together. One of my fondest memories was the day the circus came to town. Circus Flora had put on a truly marvelous spectacle under the big top, an intentional throwback to the types of shows one could imagine from a hundred years ago. Susan and Anne and I were grinning from ear to ear the entire time and we could barely contain ourselves. Meanwhile, little Charlie was just mesmerized. His mouth was agape and the look in his eyes was one of pure astonishment. It was *amazing*!

After we returned to the hostel it was time for them to hit the sack. I retired to the Pequod but soon Laura bounded into my place and asked me if I had seen the sky. I had not. She had just returned from town on her bike, and she said that she had seen some *crazy* lights from across the water and she didn't know what to make of them. I jumped up immediately and she and I headed over to the open field across the street. Mary and Nandra soon joined us.

Out from under the glare of the hostel's lights, the four of us stared out across the ocean. The stars were spectacular. It was a perfectly clear night and the Milky Way shone brightly above us. And true enough, straight ahead over the Atlantic was a very strange display of bright flashing lights. They were obviously extremely far away, but they were a striking hue of red and orange and they lit up a very well-defined space just over the horizon. They went off in spurts, probably just one or two seconds apart, and the vision was such an unusual one that none of us could quite comprehend what we were seeing.

At first we thought that it might have been Alvin and his Mothership, and then we entertained the notion of the Aurora Borealis, or the possibility of World War III just starting, but soon we surmised that what we were witnessing was a tremendous thunderstorm, many miles away, but still close enough that we could observe its violent activity. We were all completely captivated by the thought that we were experiencing such a sublime and peaceful moment, basking in the silence and the gentle ocean breezes all around us, all the while observing this terrific tempest wreaking such unknown havoc in a different reality so far away.

And as if to mark the perfect close to yet another beautiful day, a brilliant shooting star suddenly lit up the night sky like a firework directly over our heads. We all gasped.

Those midsummer days and starry nights had certainly been good to us, but the season was far from over.

Chapter 22

August

In which a bellicose red planet and a fiery month do their worst!

The purely blissful days of summer continued for quite some time, but nothing lasts forever. Eventually, Susan, Anne and Charlie had to leave us, the Milky Way drifted across the night sky in a southwesterly direction, and July turned into August.

August was a fiery month. The days had become hotter and hotter and eventually we even stopped wearing our fleeces and sweatshirts at nightfall. And the rains never really came. The last rain shower had been at the very beginning of July and it wouldn't rain again until the very end of August. When it finally did come through it wasn't nearly enough. Living on the island one became very connected to the land and the sea and the cycles of nature, and when the land became dry and parched, so did we. All the while, the bellicose red planet Mars asserted its dominance over the month as it continued to draw closer and closer to the Earth each night.

In the meantime, the crowds just wouldn't stop. It had been an incredibly busy season. When prime time hit at the beginning of the summer we were ready for it. When it continued throughout July we were up to it. But as it persisted through August it began to take its toll. It definitely took its toll on me and, after a while, I couldn't wait for it to finally be September. I always felt that the sensation of time on the island was such that every day felt like two days and that somehow the days flew by faster and faster. But by August that was no longer the case. Looking back, every day felt like at least two days, sometimes three, and they stopped flying by. The closer we got to the end of the month, the slower they seemed to churn.

The month of August brought us to the thick of summer camp season, which could eventually become quite tiresome. This year, however, the vast majority of our kids' groups had been great, mostly because there had been so many superb group leaders. I also felt that the orientation speech I gave the groups upon arrival had been finely tuned enough over the years, through a slow process of trial and error, that by now the words and the manner with which I greeted our groups had the most effective results. The expectations were clear, everyone got along and had a great time, and we had very few problems.

With the exception of the one group that arrived at midnight because there had been a bomb threat on their ferry, although they didn't bother to phone us about it, who then proceeded to burn enough food in the kitchen that they set off the fire alarm, thus waking up everyone in the entire complex, whose adult leaders literally abandoned their kids the following morning and afternoon, again without so much as a phone call or even a good explanation once they finally did show up six hours later, such that we had to continually reassure as well as feed their children, in addition to the fact that their aforementioned so-called leaders had no activities or agenda for the group during their entire stay, and that they left me with an outdoor game of fifty-two pickup on the windy afternoon when they finally rolled out three days later. (Sorry about the run-on sentence there. I needed to vent.)

But other than that, the summer camp season had been fine.

And there were lots of other good things that happened. The gentleman and superstar known as Bill stayed with us twice that summer, for a good chunk of time on both visits. At the end of his first stay, I had decided to take my one and only full day off for the season, and the two of us went off-island to visit a couple of our neighboring hostels on the mainland. We had the best time on the ferry ride discussing life, the universe and everything. And then we had an even better time visiting the other hostels, jumping into their scenes, working the crowds and promoting *our* hostel as the best in the universe! It was good fun and I think we excelled at entertaining and amusing our audiences.

By the time Bill showed up for his second visit, in the course of his adventures, he had somehow encountered and charmed a producer for a television series about the baby boom generation. The producer had then decided that he wanted to do an episode featuring Bill, as an example of a young-at-heart, fifty-something who traveled unconventionally. They picked the right guy. It was a fun day when the television crew showed up. The hostel looked great, there were some good action shots, and I even got to make a cameo appearance as we reenacted his check-in at the front desk. The two of us hammed it up for the cameras and it was really good fun.

Tales from a Hostel at the Edge of the World

At around the same time there was a lot of other excitement too. I had my first near-death experience of the month one morning when my good friend Brad, plumber extraordinaire, surprised me by showing up to make breakfast for me. Our building was very old and so were our ovens. Sometimes they could be temperamental and we were having trouble getting the pilot light started. Usually all it took was a quick flick of the lighter to get it going again. But on this occasion, for whatever reason, that tiny action resulted in a tremendous explosion of fire around my head and upper torso. I was extremely grateful for the instinctual, lightning-quick reflexes of the human body, but the sight of the oncoming explosion and the smell of my singed hair still remains burned in my skull. Needless to say, I had the ovens worked on later. And aside from almost burning myself to a crisp, Brad and I had a great visit that morning.

Shortly thereafter my parents also came out to visit for an all too brief weekend. We packed as much into it as we could amidst the heightened craziness of mid-August, but we had a lovely time. One of my fondest memories of their visit was a candle-lit outdoor barbecue we held one night, during which more and more good friends continued to arrive. Nick and Vish both brought fresh fish from the docks, including tuna, shark and striped bass, all of which were grilled to perfection. My real family got to meet my hostel family and we all enjoyed a beautiful meal and each other's company underneath the stars. Mars lurked just beneath the horizon.

August yielded some new members of the family as well. One afternoon, during that time of the day when all of the craziness of the morning had passed, all of the cleaning had been done, and before the craziness of the evening had begun, Mary, Laura, Vish and I were all sitting outside hanging out at one of the picnic tables when a car pulled up. Two strange looking characters emerged. One was tall and dark with a slick ponytail and beady eyes. The other was a young white guy wearing a long scraggly beard and the gleaming white robes and headdress of a Sikh. It tuned out that they were both musicians who were playing some gigs together on the island. Todd, the fellow with the ponytail, lived on the island, but Matthew, the soft-spoken fellow in the white turban, needed a place to stay. We didn't happen to have availability that night, but we did on the following nights, so I made a reservation for him and told him to come back the next day.

After Matthew and Todd got back into their car and drove off, the four of us could no longer resist a strange kind of laughter. Something about these two guys seemed a bit off, even for the hostel, and the whole episode just seemed vaguely bizarre. But suffice it to say that you can't judge a book by its cover. Matthew returned to the hostel the next day and he ended up being one of the coolest cats I've ever had the pleasure to know. He had been practicing kundalini yoga for many years and this path eventually led him to encounter and embrace Sikhism. And although he was intensely spiritual he was also intensely down to earth, with a sense of humor every bit as sharp as his intellect. He would often be the first one to crack a joke about his outfit and it was always delightful to hear a peaceful man in gleaming white robes casually slip the occasional expletive into a discourse. Matthew was a hell of a guy and an absolutely amazing guitarist and I was proud to count him as a friend. Todd was cool too, as well as an incredible percussionist, and the jazz these two played together was heavenly. I tried to see them perform as often as possible.

One of the saddest days of the month was the day of Vish's departure. After receiving some sudden news, Vish ended up having to return to art school much sooner than expected and, after a couple of frantic days of preparing, the hour finally came when he had to leave us. By this time, Vish had not only become a part of the family, but he was also part of the furniture. (This was actually quite literally the case, as he had left us an impressive piece of installation art in the hostel's reading room.) He definitely succeeded in having the longest tenure at the hostel. As he put it, he was a *lifer*. His presence made everything *amazing* and he would truly be missed. After we said our goodbyes, Laura and I sat down at one of the picnic tables and watched his cab drive off. "This is stupid," she commented. I agreed.

But the tide continued to ebb and flow and the good news to come was that I had arranged for our good friend Pumpkin to come join our crew. After Susan and the kids had left, Pumpkin knew that we needed extra help and so she crafted a scheme to take a sabbatical from her airline job so as to work with us for the rest of the season. We were all absolutely delighted to have her back and on board.

But even with Pumpkin on deck, every day in August just brought more and more work. And as the final days continued to churn, it all finally caught up with me and resulted in my last near-death experience of this fiery month. One of our guests had been afflicted by a terrible rash of bug bites all over her legs that were driving her crazy with itchiness. We didn't know what had caused it but obviously one possibility was the dreaded return of the bedbugs. Luciana's affliction was so intense that she eventually went to the hospital to get herself checked out. Her diagnosis ended up being an allergic reaction to sand fleas from the beach. But before her diagnosis, without knowing with certainty what had bitten her, and with all the red flags flying, I went to town on the women's dorm. I looked for every possible sign of bedbugs and found absolutely nothing, but that didn't stop me from frantically scouring the place. I vacuumed all of the cracks and crevices in all the beds, steamed out all the baseboards afresh, and after the entire room was swept immaculately clean, I mopped every inch of the floor with a mixture of soap and water and a healthy splash of insecticide.

As I was finishing I began to notice that something wasn't quite right. And after I finished it got even worse. My arms and legs felt like they were itching from the inside out and my face and ears felt like they were burning. I took a shower and it didn't help. It was bad and only getting worse. Not knowing what else to do, I jumped on my bike and rode like hell down to the hospital. And as soon as I was in triage describing the symptoms that had brought me there, a whole host of new symptoms suddenly descended upon me. I felt nauseous and I felt like I was going to pass out. Presently I vomited and passed out.

When I reemerged later the nurses had brought me to a bed where I could rest, and they were monitoring my pulse, which was fluctuating wildly. They didn't know what to make of it and neither did I. My head was still burning and I considered the possibility of malaria. I also considered the possibility of dying. It suddenly seemed like a good alternative. But the nurses soon gave me some medicine and the ordeal eventually passed. Or at least it receded enough until I was able to stand up and walk and take a cab back to the hostel. I no longer felt like dying but after I got back I ended up sleeping for sixteen hours.

When I woke up the next day I was still a bit wiped out, but on the whole I felt like a new man. All of the previous day's afflictions were essentially gone and soon I was feeling perfectly fine. I'm not entirely sure what happened but I'm sure that inhaling insecticide fumes probably had something to do with it.

Whatever it was, I survived it. I felt fully resurrected and, no less than two or three days later, we had all survived the month of August. When the first day of September finally dawned we all rejoiced. Somehow everything felt different. The weather was beautiful, the air was crisp, and the nights

Jeff Becan

were cool enough to wear our fleeces and sweatshirts again. The Halcyon days of autumn were upon us now, and not a moment too soon.

Chapter 23

Thanksgiving

In which the final season comes to an end and there is much to celebrate and be thankful for.

The final weeks of the season seemed to flit right past our eyes like a flock of piping plovers. The sun was setting earlier and earlier each evening and the last days felt both beautiful and fleeting. In fact, each day felt more fleeting than the last. And so the experience of living on an island remained ever paradoxical: autumn was largely blissful and yet fast and furious all at the same time.

September had begun with a reunion visit from my brother David that just so happened to coincide with his birthday. We did what we usually did, starting with a barbecue and ending with a great party. But this particular fete was quite exceptional in that we were joined first by our good neighbors, Robert and Jenna and Nena, and then by Matthew and Todd. Robert also happened to play a mean jazz guitar and so he and Matthew and Todd set up stage in the Pequod. It was a beautiful evening, with good company and good cheer, and sublime live music flowed all night long.

September featured another great reunion as well. Ever since my first season, my friend Heide and I had stayed in touch and so I was thrilled when I got the unexpected news that she was going to take a well-deserved break from her real job back in Germany and would be returning to the island for a short visit. This time she came with her boyfriend, Alex, who I had heard a lot about but never had the chance to meet, and he turned out to be awesome as well. Unfortunately, I wasn't able to employ them both under the table this time, but it was marvelous to catch up with Heide after more than two years, and the time I got to spend with both of them was fantastic.

The next unexpected surprise was Robert and Jenna's wedding! After many years together, and one beautiful daughter later, they had finally decided to tie the knot and it was a beautiful experience. Nandra and I were both delighted to attend. It was an outdoor ceremony at their house down the street, and they couldn't have chosen a lovelier evening. There was live music and dancing, good food and drink, and the stars were shining favorably. I had known Robert and Jenna all three seasons on the island but felt that the bonds had become stronger this year, so it was an honor to be there for the special occasion.

Towards the end of September we finally got the rain that we had needed so badly in August. What actually came through for us were the remnants of the last big hurricane. By the time it reached us there was no real threat of danger, but we still got slammed pretty hard and it was perfect. Just what the earth and our souls needed so badly. In the aftermath, one afternoon Laura and Pumpkin and I took a long walk on our beach, which had now been transformed into a different landscape entirely. For a good long time there was an enormous lake where the sand used to be, and everything had been swept entirely clean. We ended up spending hours bonding with some fun neighboring dogs and just enjoying the peace and calm that had been left in the hurricane's wake.

And as September turned into October, our final month, peace and calm returned to the hostel as well. The thick of the season was behind us now, and although we still had guests, there were now only a handful on any given day. The season was definitely coming to an end. And it remained the case that it would be my last.

Because my three years at this marvelous hostel on this enchanted island had been so rewarding, and because each season had somehow been even more beautiful than the last, but mostly because I was so grateful for such a warm atmosphere with so many marvelous people that I loved, I decided that I wanted Thanksgiving to come early this year. Before we all left the island for good, and before we would end up celebrating the real holiday with our real families, I wanted to celebrate Thanksgiving with my hostel family first.

Laura, Mary, Nandra and Pumpkin all thought this was a great idea. We picked a date and then planned and prepared and loaded up with provisions well in advance. When the day finally arrived everyone ended up contributing, but no one worked harder than Pumpkin, who probably started preparations at around seven in the morning and didn't stop until everything was ready, several hours later. It was the most sumptuous feast I had ever seen. No less than three turkeys had been prepared, several different types of stuffing and relish, and lots of secret family recipes. Robert and Jenna and Nena came over and we invited all of our guests at the time to join us as well. But the nicest surprise was that on that same day, which we had picked entirely at random, our old friend Frances also returned to the hostel, and it just so happened to be her birthday! So one celebration was happily added to another. We all had so much to be thankful for and there was no better way of expressing it than through this bountiful meal, overflowing with life and laughter and love.

* * *

Traffic continued to thin. There were now very few guests, and before long it was time to think about closing. Fortunately we were able to get a lot of work done before the final weekend, but there was still a lot left to do. And because I knew that this would be my last season, I wanted to leave the place in the best shape possible.

But one by one, the crew had to disperse. Pumpkin was the first to take her leave. She could no longer extend her sabbatical from her other job and it was finally time for her to get back to reality. Meanwhile, Nandra had decided that she would stay on the island for at least a couple more months. This meant that she would have to find someplace else to live once the hostel closed, and soon she did just that. Laura and Mary had been able to secure real jobs of their own back on the mainland, and soon they too had to leave the hostel. The nest was emptying.

The last official weekend came and went. We still had a few guests, but there was no need to send anyone away as long as I was still there. But now, in this truly remarkable place that had seen so much life over so many years, all was suddenly still and quiet. Soon the final guests of the season left and the cold and the rain began to creep in.

Meanwhile, I still had loads of work I wanted to accomplish before I was going to leave. During the previous seasons, Bill had always promised to come back for the final days but something had always come up at the last minute that prevented him. This time, however, he pulled through, and I couldn't have done it without him. Bill showed up on a cold drizzly day, saw just how much work I still wanted to get done, and he immediately jumped in to help.

The two of us started working around the clock, covering up bed frames and mattresses, washing linens and blankets, and bagging everything up for the winter. We also amassed piles of clutter and trash. We donated anything useful and tossed out everything useless. Bill also took it upon himself to clean out the tool shed in the back that had become a frightful depository of debris and detritus over the years. Over the next couple of days we created a mountain of trash out on the lawn and it was a day for rejoicing when I finally arranged for it all to be hauled off.

Earlier, as I had been cleaning out the front office, I had discovered a CD that had been hiding in one of the drawers. It was a recording of George Winston's *December* album. This was music that I had known for several years but that I hadn't listened to for quite some time. It was curious too, because I had also known that our old friend Fortune had once been involved with George Winston and that he had even written a song dedicated to her on another recording, entitled *Rainsong (Fortune's Lullaby)*. In any case, as Bill and I were tirelessly attending to the needs of our beloved hostel, that music became the most fitting soundtrack to our final days. We listened to it over and over, and it was perfectly sad and melancholy and beautiful.

And soon everything came to an end. Our work was done and the hostel had never looked better. That evening Bill and I enjoyed a good meal and a bottle of wine and we were finally able to relax and reflect. It was the end of an era and we both knew it. Somehow it felt both somber and joyful. These past three years had been such excellent years. It was sad to see them go, but it was good to celebrate them too.

The next morning Bill had to leave. And then it was just me and my hostel, the setting of so many crazy, enriching and wonderful times, and I was grateful for all of them. I spent the rest of the day revisiting the hostel, all of the nature around it, and all of the memories that will last forever. The ending of this chapter was now quite tangible. The next day I would be on a ferry back to reality, on a course set for whatever was going to come next. But somehow it now felt good to be alone, good to be able to indulge in the solitude and reflection, and to cherish it all one last time.

Afterword

Of course, I revisited the island a few times after I left the helm. How could I not? And it was always a little bittersweet. The first time was somewhat difficult emotionally. The second time, not so much. Two of the staff members, Joe and Egle, were fantastic stewards of the hostel as well as just exceptional human beings. They remain close friends to this day. A few years later, one of my best friends and I took his sailboat on an epic voyage from Northeast Harbor, Maine to Key West, Florida. Along the way, we grabbed a mooring in the town harbor, and Jackie graciously hosted us at her place in town. (Thanks again for everything, Jax!) This was off-season, but we visited the deserted hostel and it was still beautiful. The aura and spirit remained strong. Today, as of this writing at least, the state of the hostel seems to be in question and it may even end up as a piece of private property. I hope not. But whatever its future may be, I very much hope that any new owners or guests know that they are standing on very special and sacred grounds.

Made in the USA
Middletown, DE
21 June 2023

33100179R00086